Nebraska

NEBRASKA BY ROAD

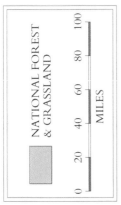

NATIONAL FOREST & GRASSLAND

MILES

100 80 60 40 20 0

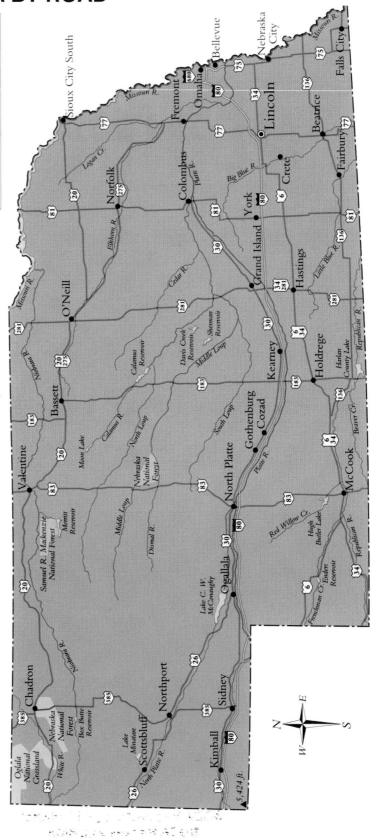

Celebrate the States

Nebraska

Ruth Bjorklund and Marlee Richards

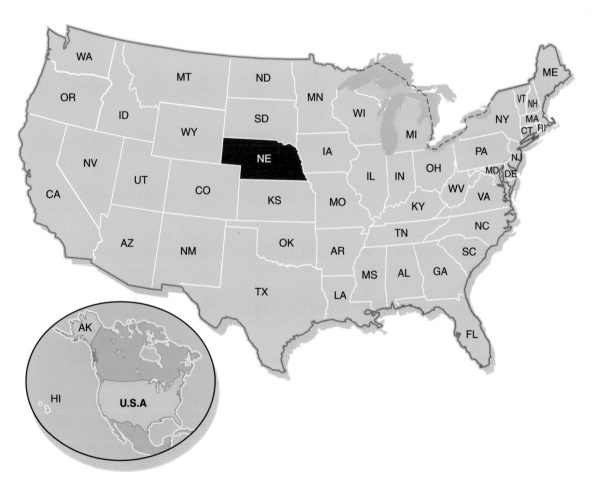

Marshall Cavendish
Benchmark
New York

Other Marshall Cavendish Offices:
Marshall Cavendish Ltd. 5th Floor, 32-38 Saffron Hill, London EC1N 8 FH, UK • Marshall Cavendish International (Asia) Private Limited, 1 New Industrial Road, Singapore 536196 • Marshall Cavendish International (Thailand) Co Ltd. 253 Asoke, 12th Flr, Sukhumvit 21 Road, Klongtoey Nua, Wattana, Bangkok 10110, Thailand • Marshall Cavendish (Malaysia) Sdn Bhd, Times Subang, Lot 46, Subang Hi-Tech Industrial Park, Batu Tiga, 40000 Shah Alam, Selangor Darul Ehsan, Malaysia

Marshall Cavendish is a trademark of Times Publishing Limited

All websites were available and accurate when this book was sent to press.

Library of Congress Cataloging-in-Publication Data

Bjorklund, Ruth.
Nebraska / by Ruth Bjorklund and Marlee Richards.—2nd edition
p. cm. — (Celebrate the states)
Summary: "Provides comprehensive information on the geography, history, wildlife, governmental structure, economy, cultural diversity, peoples, religion, and landmarks of Nebraska"—Provided by publisher.
Includes bibliographical references and index.
ISBN 978-0-7614-4732-0
1. Nebraska—Juvenile literature. I. Richards, Marlee. II. Title.

F666.3.B58 2011
978.2—dc22
2009002600

Editor: Christine Florie
Co-Editor: Denise Pangia
Publisher: Michelle Bisson
Art Director: Anahid Hamparian
Series Designer: Adam Mietlowski

Photo research and layout by Marshall Cavendish International (Asia) Private Limited—
Thomas Khoo, Benson Tan and Gu Jing

Cover Photo by Corbis

The photographs in this book are used by permission and through the courtesy of; *Photolibrary/Alamy*: back cover, 26, 44, 46, 51, 57, 76, 92, 130, 131, 134, 135, 136, 137; *Photolibrary*: 11, 14, 17, 25, 27, 30, 49, 61, 64, 74, 84, 86, 105 (top), 114; *National Geographic Society Image Collection*: 12, 19, 22, 82, 88, 95, 105 (bottom), 116; *Corbis*: 8, 13, 31, 35, 37, 41, 96, 101, 103, 109, 118, 119, 122, 124, 125, 129, 132; *Jafe Parsons*: 21; *Getty Images*: 29, 55, 60, 62, 78, 117, 120, 121, 126; *Joe Wicks, Grand Island, Nebraska*: 47; *AP Photo*: 53, 79, 115, 123; *alt.TYPE/REUTERS*: 67; *TopFoto*: 68; *Lonely Planet Images*: 90, 133.

Printed in Malaysia
1 3 5 6 4 2

Contents

Nebraska Is . . .

Nebraska is a land of strange beauty . . .

"She had never known before how much the country meant to her. The chirping of the insects in the long grass had been like the sweetest music. She had felt as if her heart were hiding down there, somewhere, with the quail and the plover and all the little wild things that crooned or buzzed in the sun. Under the long shaggy ridge, she felt the future stirring."

—Willa Cather, *O Pioneers!*

. . . where the environment yields unusual treasures.

"The Surrounding Plains are open void of timber and level to a great extent; hence the wind from whatever quarter it may blow, drives with unusual force over the naked plains and against this hill; . . . from the top of this mound we beheld a most beautiful landscape."

—Meriwether Lewis and William Clark, explorers

"One thing we have is native prairie. This part of the country used to be grassland. So some may think it looks boring, but it's actually kind of beautiful if you get to know plants and grasses and wildflowers."

—Molly Klocksin, counselor and reporter

Nebraskans possess special qualities.

"Many fine Americans were born in such holes [sod houses] in the earth: senators, oil magnates, doctors, writers, stockmen and preachers—all kinds of people."

—Mari Sandoz, author

"The openness of rural Nebraska certainly influenced me. That openness, in a way, fosters the imagination."

—Matthew Sweet, musician

They value each other and their state's history.

"I have traveled a lot, and I will say Nebraska is very welcoming. There are a lot of people who love to share state history."

—Diane Thomas, singer and hotel owner

"From original homestead cabins to blazing gunfights, from architectural wonders to ethnic festivals, from the Pony Express to the Oregon Trail, the Land of Pioneers is a rich and exciting place to discover."

—Hannah McNally, travel writer

They treasure their homeland.

"It is beautiful . . . in the memories of the Nebraska-born whose dwelling in far places has given them moments of homesickness for the low rolling hills, the swell and dip of the ripening wheat, the fields of sinuously waving corn and the elusively fragrant odor of alfalfa."

—Bess Streeter Aldrich, author

"I have lived in this state my whole life, yet I never cease to be amazed by its beauty and its people. Nebraska is still the great, open land of new horizons that the Native Americans knew, and its people are still as open as those horizons."

—Ben Nelson, former Nebraska governor and current U.S. senator

Nebraska is a state that combines worldly big cities with country charm. Larger cities offer vivacity and business opportunities. Open land, especially in the west, provides a home to crops, cattle, and down-home living. Nebraska midwesterners cherish family and their varied pioneer heritage. They value their safe, affordable communities, rich history, and interesting environment. More than anything, Nebraskans look to a promising future.

Chapter One

Where the West Begins

Four million years ago the land that became Nebraska sat under a great inland sea. Later, glaciers moved from the northeast into part of the state. They melted into fast-flowing waters. This pattern occurred three different times over the next hundreds of millions of years. Melting glaciers and seas leveled much of the land. In some places they carved riverbeds and unusual landforms.

WHERE IS NEBRASKA?

Today, Nebraska looms large across the middle of North America, making it the sixteenth largest state. It shares boundaries with South Dakota in the north, Kansas in the south, Iowa and Missouri in the east, and Colorado and Wyoming in the west.

Early pioneers considered central North America, including Nebraska Territory, the West. Their definition of the West changed as emigrants explored new regions beyond the Missouri River. Once settlers reached the Pacific Ocean, the region that included Nebraska became known as the Midwest. Nebraska remains a midwestern state, although one of the most

Scotts Bluff Monument preserves 3,000 acres of unusual land formations that rise over the otherwise flat prairie land below.

western ones. At one time the Nebraska tourist office claimed the state was "where the West begins."

THE DISSECTED TILL PLAINS

The last glaciers to retreat from northeastern Nebraska left behind gently rolling hills. Soil in the hills contain a fertile mix of sand, gravel, and clay—or till. Geologists call this easternmost part of Nebraska the Dissected Till Plains. The region included broad grasslands, sand dunes, jagged rocks, and racing rivers.

Melting glaciers carved the state's three major riverbeds. Two flow through eastern Nebraska. The Missouri River lines the state's eastern and northeastern border. The Missouri, once nicknamed the Mighty Mo, has been slowed by dams. But along the section that lies in northeast Nebraska, the river runs wild past fertile riverbanks, scenic bluffs, and woodlands. Farther south the glaciers left large salt marshes in addition to rivers. Shorebirds, such as black terns and yellowlegs, still flock to the green and marshy areas of southeastern Nebraska.

The Platte River runs west to east into the Missouri River. The Platte cuts through the heart of Nebraska. Eastern Nebraska, south of the Platte River, is often called Willa Cather country. A daughter of early pioneers, the famed author Willa Cather saw only a few trees alongside rivers and streams. Elsewhere she noticed an endless ocean of grass. Cather later wrote, "Trees were so rare in that country . . . that we used to feel anxious about them and visit them as if they were persons."

Today, towns and farms have replaced the native prairie grass. But the sound of crickets, the stunning color of wildflowers, and an occasional glimpse of the greater prairie chicken still recall the magnificent prairies that once covered the region.

Nebraska's Dissected Till Plains is a region of smooth, rolling hills.

CENTRAL NEBRASKA

South-central Nebraska contains the Big Bend Reach of the Platte River. An Oto and Omaha Indian word meaning "flat water," Platte is an apt name. It has long been described as "a mile wide, an inch deep, and uphill all the way." The Platte starts high in the Rocky Mountains as two rivers, the North Platte and the South Platte. The rivers join in western Nebraska, flowing as one great river across the state. Dams and irrigation canals have reduced the Platte to less than half its original depth everywhere in this section. Silty sandbars, wayward currents, and abundant croplands create a paradise for birds that feed on grubs, snails, and corn. The world's largest flock of sandhill cranes migrate here annually to fatten up before heading to Canada and Russia to nest. Millions of geese as well as mallard, merganser, and pintail ducks join the cranes each spring.

Each spring nearly half a million cranes gather on the Platte River in central Nebraska during their northward migration.

RESTORING PLATTE RIVER HABITATS

Efforts to protect habitat along the Platte River began in 1978 with the Whooping Crane Maintenance Trust. Since that time 10,000 acres of river habitat have been reclaimed. In 2006 another major effort began. Biologists realized that the central Platte River needed restoration. Otherwise the state would lose many endangered birds and other wildlife completely. Wildlife experts asked state, federal, and private groups to donate money to buy and restore a 200-acre piece of land near the Iain Nicolson Audubon Center at Rowe Sanctuary on the central Platte River. At one time the region was home to whooping cranes. By 2006 the site had lost great numbers of cranes and other endangered birds, which hadn't returned to the area in ten years.

After renewal began, workers removed trees, cleared and sculpted the riverbed, and built nesting islands. They hoped the cleaning and improvements would restore the river to its former state, one that would attract threatened wildlife species. Within a year biologists announced that their plan proved successful. They discovered ten nests of the least tern and two of the piping plover (right), both endangered species. The instant success encouraged expansion of the project. Meanwhile, state biologists continue to monitor the numbers of fish, birds, and other wildlife for signs of return and multiplication.

The Niobrara River, one of the last free-flowing rivers of the Great Plains, runs across northern Nebraska. This river valley contains exceptionally rich natural resources. Eastern and western trees merge along its banks. Eastern trees, such as bur oak and birch, stop reproducing west of Nebraska, while the western ponderosa pines end their eastern pollination in this area. A variety of animals roam the lush region.

The Niobrara River runs through northern Nebraska, a region lush with wildlife.

Among them are Texas longhorn cattle, prairie dogs, white-tailed deer, and burrowing owls. Buffalo and elk range freely in the Fort Niobrara National Wildlife Refuge.

Covering most of north-central Nebraska is the extraordinary region called the Sandhills. This plain contains the largest expanse of sand in the Western Hemisphere and forms dunes as high as 300 feet. Roots of wild grasses anchor the sand in place. Unlike other sandy areas of the world, the Sandhills include many natural lakes and streams. These provide homes for varied forms of wildlife. According to one local resident, "The Sandhills lakes may not be very deep, but they sure hold a lot of fish." In addition, birds such as teals, loons, and the rare Clark's grebes flock to the Sandhills. Bald and golden eagles soar overhead as deer, antelope, and coyotes roam the land. Few people and roads exist in the region, but its grassy carpet provides an ideal environment for grazing cattle and buffalo. As a result the Sandhills is dotted with hundreds of large ranches.

Another feature of the Sandhills is the Nebraska National Forest. The Dismal and Loup rivers flow past the only planted forest in the National Forest System. According to historians, a University of Nebraska professor began experimenting with planting cedars and pines. He hoped that growing a timber supply would encourage people to settle in the Sandhills. The forest would provide income for the settlers and feed the nation's hunger for lumber, which was decimating the natural forests. His plan never succeeded in attracting settlers, but the resulting patch of green became a magnet for songbirds, sharp-tailed grouse, wild turkeys, and prairie chickens.

LAND AND WATER

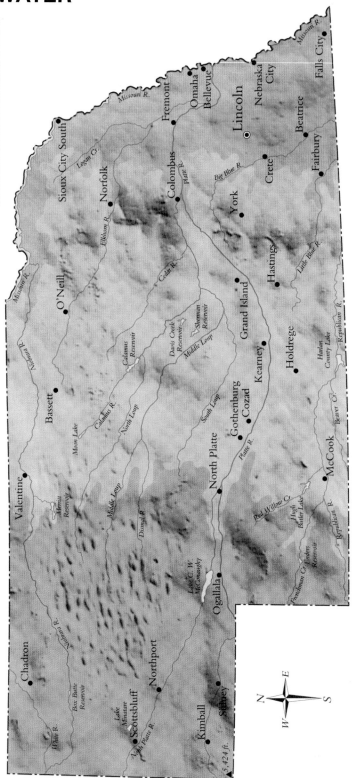

THE PANHANDLE

Nebraska's windswept Panhandle points westward beyond the fertile prairies like the handle of a pan. This western region of the state transforms from high plains in the south to unusual formations of pine-covered buttes and badlands in the north. When early pioneers first spied this land, they were amazed. In his book *The Gathering of Zion*, author Wallace Stegner wrote, "They had penetrated into a new world of strange forms, strange colorings, parching air, deceptive distances: buffalo country, horned-toad country, wolf country—the authentic West."

Wind, water, and sandstorms carved giant sandstone and siltstone buttes in the Panhandle. Chimney Rock towers 315 feet above the Platte River. The tall column of clay, sandstone, and volcanic ash once stood as a beacon for nineteenth-century pioneers traveling west on the Oregon-California Trail. A slow-moving wagon train could look across

The 315-foot-tall Chimney Rock provided a marker for settlers traveling west along the Oregon Trail.

the plains and see the spire days before reaching it. Farther west sits a towering formation called Scotts Bluff. Plains tribes called it *Me-a-pa-te*, meaning "the hill that is hard to go around."

North of Scotts Bluff is the most rugged area of Nebraska, the Pine Ridge region. Jagged white cliffs and ponderosa pines shelter buffalo, elk, and bighorn sheep. These animals have been rescued from near extinction and reintroduced onto this magnificent land. Farther north is the Oglala National Grassland, an eerie landscape of rock formations and short grasses.

Buried deep beneath central and western Nebraska lies the Oglala Aquifer, a gigantic pool of underground water stretching from South Dakota to Texas. The aquifer formed 10,000 to 25,000 years ago, when the sand and gravel beds under the plains absorbed and stored water running off the Rocky Mountains. Inventive settlers discovered that a pump driven by a windmill could bring the Oglala Aquifer's life-giving water to the surface. They named this vast resource after the town of Oglala, Nebraska, in 1899.

WINDS OF CHANGE

Winds from the southeast carry warm sea air from the Gulf of Mexico across the continent. Temperatures on the ground warm the air even more as it moves northward overhead. By the time airstreams reach Nebraska, temperatures are high. Nebraskans often find summer temperatures reach between 90 and 100 degrees Fahrenheit. The hottest recorded temperature was 118 °F, in Minden in 1936. In the winter, wind directions shift, and cold weather blows in from the northwest. In 1989 Oshkosh registered a frigid –47 °F, a low point for Nebraskans.

Springtime brings wild and unpredictable weather to Nebraska.

Hundred-degree summer days or frigid, wintry ice storms may be newsworthy. But the wildest weather in Nebraska comes in springtime, when weather can be brutal and unpredictable. Warm winds from the south sweep across the plains as chilly winds from the north bear down. When these weather fronts clash, anything can happen. Lightning, thunder, tornadoes, floods, and hail can strike at a moment's notice and change a pleasant afternoon into a run-for-cover tempest. Autumn, too, varies in extremes. Heather Kreifel of Nebraska City says, "You never know what to expect. Yesterday my kids went to school in shorts. Today they have on winter coats."

BALANCING NATURE

Like other states, Nebraska struggles to balance the needs of residents, farmers, ranchers, and wildlife in the use of land, water, and other natural resources. For example, all major rivers in the state except the Niobrara are dammed. Dams play an important role in flood control and help farmers irrigate their fields. But they often harm fish, birds, and other animals.

Many creatures thrive near rivers where the water flows naturally, forming slow-moving backwater pools and sloughs. Dams and man-made channels have eliminated this habitat, threatening many of the state's endangered animals, such as the whooping crane, river otter, and Eskimo curlew.

Farms, towns, and cities have altered Nebraska forever. Prairies have been plowed under, woodlands cut down, and wetlands drained. Some animals, such as the grizzly bear, the gray wolf, and the ruffed grouse, could not survive Nebraska's settlement and have disappeared completely.

In 2009 Kent Ullberg installed his wildlife sculpture, called *Spirit of Nebraska's Wilderness*, in downtown Omaha. The nine-block, multiple-piece bronze project pays tribute to the state's heritage. In the display a wagon train stampedes a herd of larger-than-life buffalo and a flock of fifty-eight geese. "When humans entered the wilderness, they disturbed wildlife and this is a symbol: we are displacing the buffalo, and the geese and the animals are running," Ullberg said.

In 1992 Nebraskans voted for a state lottery to help save wildlife and the environment. Half of the lottery's income goes to the Nebraska

Kent Ullberg's wildlife sculpture called the Spirit of Nebraska's Wilderness *spans nine blocks in downtown Omaha.*

Environmental Trust. Anyone with a plan to restore a stream, plant a small forest, or recycle waste products can apply to the trust for funding. This unique method of protecting the environment is straightforward and effective, just like the resourceful citizens of Nebraska.

Chapter Two

Land of Possibilities

"The openness of rural Nebraska certainly influenced me," said musician Matthew Sweet. "That openness, in a way, fosters the imagination." Even as the land experienced change, people throughout the centuries have found Nebraska a place to live, prosper, and imagine exciting possibilities.

THE FIRST PEOPLE

After the last major glacier retreated 9,000 to 12,000 years ago, the Paleo-Indians became the first humans to arrive in the Nebraska region. They used stone spears as weapons to hunt and butcher wild beasts for food. Their prey included giant buffalo, ground sloths, and mammoths—relatives of today's elephants. Hunters followed the animals from place to place. Because of the constant hunt for food, families lived in temporary camps rather than permanent homes.

About 13,000 years ago the climate began to change. Watering holes dried up, destroying trees and other vegetation. Camels, horses, mammoths, and other Ice Age mammals disappeared. Natives continued

Pioneers traveled along the Oregon Trail through Nebraska's flatland.

to hunt animals for food, but they gathered wild plants to supplement the smaller animals they found. These early people moved with their food sources but returned to previous campsites each year.

Around two thousand years ago woodland peoples moved to the area from eastern forests. They hunted and crafted tools of bone and, for the first time, formed clay pots. Woodlanders dug their dwellings into the earth and supported them with poles covered with animal skins. Families constructed these homes in small villages and buried their dead in earthen mounds. For part of the year they lived together, planting small farms with beans and corn.

Between 1200 and 1450 CE, the ancestors of some modern Nebraska tribes enjoyed a period of peace and prosperity. About 1,200 people settled into villages. They farmed and produced decorative pottery. They traded with distant coastal civilizations and created ornaments from seashells. But in the late fourteenth century, terrific dust storms and droughts drove them from the region. Archaeologists believe the central Great Plains remained almost unoccupied for about two hundred years.

By the mid to late 1500s the ancestors of the Pawnee tribe had settled in what is now Nebraska. Their many villages hugged the banks of the Platte River. The Pawnee built earthen lodges constructed of poles covered with brush and packed dirt. Men hunted over a wide range. Women tended fields of corn, squash, beans, and melon, and gathered wild potatoes growing near the river. In summer and autumn the entire village hunted buffalo. Taking their homes—cone-shaped tepees made of buffalo skins and poles—the Pawnee moved their belongings on large frames dragged by dogs. After the hunt the people returned to their farms to harvest their crops, fish in nearby waters, and use the buffalo for food, shelter, clothing, tools, and weapons.

Buffalo provided the Plains Indians with food and resources for shelter, weapons, tools, and clothing.

A PAWNEE CREATION MYTH

The Plains Indians hold deep spiritual ties to nature. Black Elk, a Lakota holy man, explains, "Is not the sky a father and the earth a mother, and are not all living things with feet or wings or roots their children?" Here is a creation myth of the Pawnee:

Once long ago, all things slept underground, waiting. There were herds of buffalo, antelope, wolves, rabbits, birds, and people. Then the Buffalo Woman awoke and walked among the creatures. As she passed, people and animals opened their eyes. She touched all, even those farthest from her. Suddenly, she bowed her head and stepped away. In her place was a blinding light. Animals rose up to follow her, first a young cow, then a buffalo, then another and another, each, for a moment, standing alone in the light. The people arose, old and young. They all stepped onto the green grassy earth, along the Platte River, under a blue sky filled with birds. The buffalo scattered about the prairie, and the people moved in every direction. Together, they knew that they were meant to share this place called Earth.

EUROPEANS ARRIVE

At one time historians believed the first Europeans in Nebraska were Spanish explorers led by Francisco Vásquez de Coronado. However, recent research shows that Coronado went only as far north as central Kansas.

In 1541 the Spanish ventured across the plains searching for Quivira, a legendary city made of gold. Instead of gold, Coronado, as he described it, found "little villages, and in many of these they do not plant anything and do not have any houses except of skins and sticks, and they wander around with the cows." The cows turned out to be buffalo.

Fifty years later the French landed in North America. The first Europeans to visit the region that is now Nebraska were probably Spanish and French explorers, fur trappers, and adventurers.

By the early eighteenth century, tribes living farther east, such as the Oto, Omaha, Missouri, and Ponca, had begun migrating into what is now Nebraska. Like the Pawnee, they were farmers who lived in earthen lodges and hunted buffalo for part of the year. To the west, nomadic tribes wandered year-round. The Lakota Cheyenne, Arapaho, Comanche, and Kiowa immigrated to the Nebraska region from the east or south and followed buffalo herds and raided other tribes' settlements.

The Europeans' arrival changed the lives of American Indians forever. The plains were rich in buffalo, beaver, deer, mink, and elk. Spanish and French traders established trading posts along the Platte, Niobrara, and Missouri rivers. The traders received hides and fur from the native hunters in exchange for horses, guns,

American Indians bartered their furs in exchange for goods.

beads, sugar, cloth, metal implements, and sometimes whiskey—all of which altered the Indian way of life. Horses and guns made the Indians more efficient hunters. These items also made the Indians tougher to fight in battle. Some of the manufactured goods Indians received in trade made their lives easier. Although it was illegal, alcohol was a common trade item; it damaged Indians' lives and cultures. Worse, the white newcomers brought diseases previously unknown to the Indians. Many native people lost their lives to these strange illnesses.

THE GROWING NATION

While American Indians and European traders harvested the bounty of the land, foreign governments competed for ownership of the area. Treaties and warfare shifted custody of the Great Plains between Spain and France. During that time the United States formed a government to the east.

In 1803 France and the United States agreed to a land sale known as the Louisiana Purchase. The arrangement granted all land between the Mississippi River and the Rocky Mountains and from Canada to the Gulf of Mexico to the United States. As a result of this sale, the young nation doubled in size.

President Thomas Jefferson sent representatives to explore the new land. Within a year of the purchase, he commissioned Meriwether Lewis and William Clark to lead an expedition up the Missouri River and west to the Pacific Ocean. Their mission was to map, chart, and report scientific and geographic findings, seek a water route across the continent, and make contact with native tribes.

On August 3, 1804, high on a bluff above the Missouri River, the explorers held council with representatives of the Oto and Missouri tribes.

During the meeting Lewis and Clark offered gifts of tobacco, roasted meat, and flour to tribal chiefs who in return gave the Americans watermelons. On the site now known as Council Bluff, Lewis and Clark informed the chiefs about the change in government. At that time the chiefs found no reason to feel threatened by the news. They invited the Americans to cross their lands in peace.

Two years later Governor James Wilkinson sent Lieutenant Zebulon Pike to the Great Plains. In his report Pike declared that the area was made of "barren soil, parched and dried up for eight months in the year." Considering the reports, the U.S. Congress saw little value in the territory and in 1834 declared it "Indian Country." Most whites were prohibited from settling west of the Missouri River. Only trappers, traders, soldiers, and missionaries were allowed. The settlers constructed the first permanent white settlement at Bellevue near present-day Omaha, in 1823.

Bellevue was the first permanent white settlement in Nebraska.

THE GREAT PLATTE RIVER ROAD

Although whites were prohibited from settling in what would be Nebraska, they did travel across the land. Fur traders and missionaries came first. Before long, thousands of settlers and gold seekers traveled in wagons or on foot along what the Indians called the Great Platte River Road. The pioneers headed west to the Rockies and then to Oregon, Utah, or California. The wide, flat valley provided an easy route to travel with oxen or horses pulling loaded wagons. Between 1841 and 1866 up to 500,000 pioneers followed the Platte. So many settlers emigrated along this highway that General William T. Sherman determined it had three virtues: "It was dry, it was level, and it went in exactly the right direction."

Settlers traveled in covered wagons along the Platte River Road in northeast Nebraska.

The Homestead Act brought hundreds of settlers into Nebraska territory after 1862.

SETTLING THE TERRITORY

In 1854 Nebraska became a U.S. territory. This meant that whites could settle the region. Businesspeople started a land grab, creating towns almost overnight. Omaha exploded into the territory's largest city, with a population of about one hundred people. Eight years later, in 1862, Congress passed the Homestead Act. This law allowed settlers to claim 160 acres each for a small fee. After working the land for five years, a homesteader would own the land outright. The first person to take advantage of the Homestead Act was a native Nebraskan, Daniel Freeman, who staked his claim on January 1, 1863.

THE KINKAIDERS

In an effort to attract farmers to western Nebraska, Congressman Moses P. Kinkaid introduced a bill passed in 1904 for the creation of 640-acre homesteads in western Nebraska. Most "Kinkaiders" failed, and their claims were incorporated into large ranches that are typical of that part of Nebraska today. Still, sometimes Kinkaid was hailed in song for helping homesteaders settle the Sandhills.

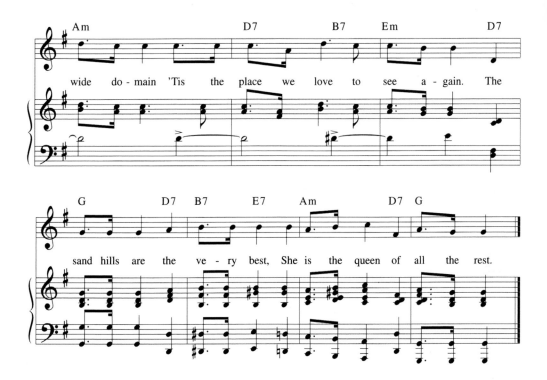

wide do-main 'Tis the place we love to see a-gain. The

sand hills are the ve-ry best, She is the queen of all the rest.

The corn we raise is our delight,
The melons, too, are out of sight.
Potatoes grown are extra fine,
And can't be beat in any clime.
Chorus

The peaceful cows in pastures dream,
And furnish us with golden cream.
So I shall keep my Kinkaid home,
And never far away shall roam.

Final chorus
Then let us all with hearts sincere,
Thank him for what has brought us here,
And for the homestead law he made,
The noble Moses P. Kinkaid.

Although homesteaders were enthusiastic about Nebraska Territory, some of its driest regions, such as the Sandhills and the Panhandle, attracted few settlers. The land seemed suitable for raising livestock, but it took 20 acres of wild grass to feed one cow. That meant ranchers needed more than 160 acres to earn a living. In 1904 Congress passed the Kinkaid Act, which allowed the creation of 640-acre homesteads in western Nebraska. Most failed in the Sandhills, so the Kinkaid lands passed into the hands of ranchers. By 1917 all public lands had been claimed.

From 1861 to 1865 the U.S. Civil War between Northern free states and Southern slave states raged. Most Nebraskans were against slavery. In 1861 the U.S. legislature passed a law banning slavery in Nebraska, even though only a handful of slaves were even brought to Nebraska. A few slaves from Missouri made their way north to freedom along a western branch of a secret network of hiding places known as the Underground Railroad.

After the North defeated the South in 1865 and the Civil War ended, more Americans looked west for their future. A few businesspeople envisioned building a railroad that would carry passengers across the continent. To help with the enormous cost of such an undertaking, Congress gave the Union Pacific Railroad huge parcels of land along the route, which included Nebraska. Beginning in 1865 workers laid 265 miles of track across Nebraska. Boomtowns sprang up along the route.

By the time Nebraska became a state on March 1, 1867, the Union Pacific Railroad stretched from Omaha to North Platte and would soon reach the state's western border. To raise money, railroad companies began selling off the extra land Congress had given them. They advertised, "You only have to tickle [the land] with a plow and it will laugh a harvest that will gladden your hearts." People swarmed into the new state.

RESETTLING AMERICAN INDIANS

As settlers flooded into Nebraska after 1854, the government forced American Indians to give up their lands and move to small reservations. The government repeatedly broke treaties with the tribes. Meanwhile, the great herds of buffalo disappeared. White hunters had slaughtered the buffalo almost to extinction. Without their most important source of food and with their population weakened by disease, many American Indians left their ancestral homes. Entire villages moved onto reservations set up by the U.S. government in order to survive.

Even after most Nebraska tribes had moved to reservations, however, whites refused to leave the remaining ones alone. In 1877 the U.S. government uprooted the Ponca tribe, living on the Niobrara River, and ordered them to Indian Territory, now Oklahoma. Because tribal members resisted, the government agreed to allow a party of chiefs to go in advance and judge the worthiness of the new reservation. However, once the chiefs reached the new reservation, soldiers imprisoned them. But one winter night they escaped. For fifty days the chiefs traveled on foot, scavenging for food and sleeping unprotected on the cold ground. Once back home, they reported the harsh treatment they had received. The Ponca voted not to move, but soldiers forced them anyway.

Standing Bear was a chief of the Ponca Indian tribe that was relocated to Indian Territory in 1877.

The new reservation provided little food and no shelter. Within two years, a third of the Ponca tribe had died. Chief Standing Bear, grieving for the loss of his son, vowed to return to Nebraska to bury the dead. After a bitter ten-week journey, Standing Bear and thirty members of his tribe reached their homeland. Soldiers arrested the chief and brought him to Fort Omaha. At his trial Standing Bear told the court, "If a white man had land and someone should swindle him, that man would try and get it back, and you would not blame him. Look on me. Take pity on me, and help me save the lives of the women and children."

The judge freed Standing Bear and declared, "An Indian is a person within the meaning of the law." This was the first time a court had ruled that an Indian had legal rights. Standing Bear was allowed to live out his life in Nebraska.

Though some tribes trusted the U.S. government, many resented losing their land. They engaged in skirmishes with white settlers. The government established outposts at forts Kearny, McPherson, Hartsuff, Sidney, Robinson, and Atkinson to protect the settlers.

From 1855 through the late 1870s periodic fighting between Indians and whites in Nebraska and elsewhere became known as the Indian Wars. One of the most famous battles during the wars occurred at Little Bighorn in Montana in 1876. General George Custer lost to Lakota warriors under the command of Sitting Bull and Crazy Horse. Afterward, the U.S. Army forced thousands of Lakota to give up their weapons and move onto reservations. The next year Crazy Horse brought two thousand of his people with him to Fort Robinson and asked for peace, but soldiers killed him. In the winter of 1878 a band of Cheyenne under Chief Dull Knife escaped from an Oklahoma reservation and trekked a snowy 600 miles to Nebraska. On January 9, 1879, they were captured near Fort Robinson. Soldiers killed most of them, too. Historians agree that on that night the last American Indians to resist had been defeated.

O PIONEERS!

For the pioneers Nebraska was a harsh new world. In *Sandhill Sundays*, homesteader Mari Sandoz wrote, "No pleasantness here to sun-blinded eyes. Only a little valley carpeted with russet bunchgrass tucked in between towering hills whose highest dunes are bald among clusters of green-black yuccas. Decidedly no home." The desolate landscape motivated the first homesteaders to settle as close as they could to the riverbanks, where the only trees grew.

Once most river valley land was taken, settlers staked claims on the treeless prairie. Without timber for constructing houses, barns, and fences, the pioneers had to find other materials. They cut hard, packed sod into slabs and built houses. These houses, called soddies, suited the rigors of prairie life. They stayed cool in summer and warm in winter. Small and

Packed sod houses, called soddies, protected against harsh weather on Nebraska's prairie.

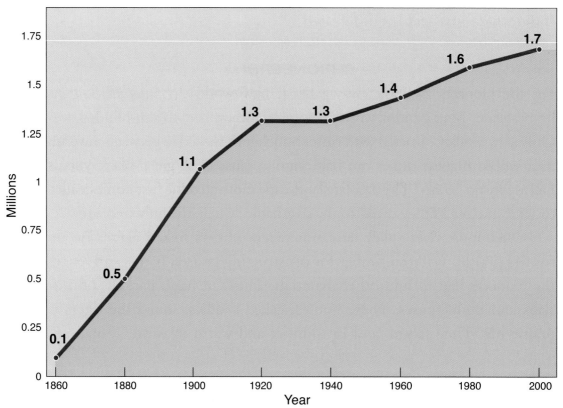

POPULATION GROWTH: 1860–2000

close to the ground, they sheltered their inhabitants against high winds and tornadoes better than wood houses. But they leaked, and mice and snakes easily squeezed through cracks in the sod. Settlers jokingly called the sod "Nebraska marble."

Despite challenges, the early settlers persisted. On the rolling eastern prairies, farmers grew corn and wheat. On the western plains, ranchers raised horses, cattle, and sheep. Though people were hopeful, life was rarely easy. In 1873 and 1874 a severe drought ruined all the crops. And if that was not hardship enough, a plague of grasshoppers followed the drought. A newspaper columnist in Osceola, Nebraska, reported,

The air is filled with [grasshoppers], the ground is covered with them, and people think and talk of nothing else. It rains grasshoppers, and snows grasshoppers. We cannot walk the streets without being struck in the face and eyes by grasshoppers, and we cannot sleep for dreaming grasshoppers, and if the little devils do not leave for some other clime soon, we shall go grasshopper crazy.

Some people did leave the land, but many more stayed. Before the Civil War began, the population of Nebraska was 28,841. Ten years later it reached four times that number. By 1900 the population had climbed to more than one million. Never again did Nebraska grow at such a pace.

CHANGING LIFE ON THE FARM

During the 1880s ample rainfall enabled farmers to raise large crops. But other elements took their toll on profits. Railroads charged steep shipping fees to send goods to market, and banks imposed high interest payments on money they loaned to farmers for seed and equipment. Many farmers chose to fight these unfair costs by forming new political groups. The first, called the Farmers Alliance, later became the Populist Party. Many reforms resulted from Populist causes, such as limiting banking and shipping fees. Because of the Populist reforms and favorable weather, Nebraska farmers prospered in the early 1900s.

The era of prosperity and hope ended in 1914 with the outbreak of World War I in Europe. In 1917 the United States joined Great Britain and its allies in their war against Germany and its allies. This was a difficult time for Nebraska's many German immigrants. In America some people felt threatened by anything German. German words such as *sauerkraut* and *wiener* were changed to *liberty cabbage* and *hot dog*. German farmers in Nebraska were encouraged to speak only English and to become American citizens.

During the war more than 57,000 Nebraskans served in the military. Meanwhile, back home the government supported farmers with the slogan "Wheat will win the war!" Prices increased, and Nebraskans harvested record crops.

The war ended, and it seemed as if a new era of agricultural prosperity had arrived. Tractors and combines replaced horse-drawn farm machinery. Electricity and roads reached isolated farms and rural villages. When the economy soured between 1929 and 1939, Nebraska farmers did not suffer as much as others at first. Their wealth was in land rather than in stocks and business deals.

But the 1930s ushered in a crushing drought that ruined crops and changed everyday life. Clouds of dust swirled across the plains during what became known as the Dust Bowl era. Retired music teacher Ann Peterson recalls, "The dust was so bad it was gray the whole day. Morning the same as night." Many farmers could not survive the drought. More than 65,000 Nebraskans packed their belongings and left for California and a better life. They abandoned more than 600,000 acres of Nebraska farmland.

By the time rain fell again at the end of the decade, farmers had learned a few lessons. Their most valuable resource, their soil, had dried up and blown away. It was time to conserve. Farmers planted trees to slow the wind and hold the earth in place. They rotated crops to keep the soil healthy. They used water more carefully. Slowly, the soil healed.

During the 1930s drought dried up Nebraska farms, forcing many to leave their home state.

FROM FARMING TO INDUSTRY

In 1941 war interrupted progress again. Thousands of Nebraska farm boys enlisted in the military and went off to fight in World War II. Those who didn't join farmed the fields to produce food for people at home and abroad. Men and women worked in factory assembly lines that switched from making farm products to manufacturing weapons and machinery. At the Martin Bomber Plant located on the Offutt Air Force Base outside of Omaha, factory workers built military planes, including the *Enola Gay* and the *Bockscar*. These two B-29s carried the atomic bombs dropped on Japan that ended the war.

After the war Offutt Air Force Base, a former frontier outpost, grew in international importance. In 1948 the federal government made Offutt the new Strategic Air Command (SAC) headquarters. SAC was the technical command center of the U.S. Air Force. In 1992 SAC was replaced with the U.S. Strategic Command, or STRATCOM, that oversees all the nation's air, land, and naval nuclear forces. The United States controls its nuclear arsenal from deep underground at Offutt in Omaha. Because SAC and STRATCOM required the most advanced technology, Omaha has become a national center for telecommunications.

More recently, the state government has targeted specific industries to encourage business growth throughout the state. The emphasis on new business has resulted in a 30-percent population increase. Nebraska's two major cities, Omaha and Lincoln, have flourished.

Nebraska's location in the middle of the nation contributed to the state becoming a transportation and communication center. Interstate 80 now cuts through 482 miles of the state and is one of the busiest

U.S. highways. Seven north-south highways and two major rail systems have allowed Nebraska to become a leader in warehousing and transporting goods.

Nebraska also boasts electricity rates that are 42 percent lower than the U.S. average, and the state owns the public utilities. This means the state offers low-cost power to run telecommunication and other businesses.

Technological advances such as irrigation, fertilizer, and hybrid seeds also helped improve farming techniques. The 55,000 farms and ranches in Nebraska are some of the most successful in the world. Farming feeds a lively food-processing industry that is assisted by University of Nebraska research. Ranching and cattle feeding have supported Nebraska's leading role in the meatpacking industry, particularly in Dawson and Dakota counties. These industries provide low-skilled jobs that attract great numbers of foreign-born workers to low-wage jobs. These newcomers want what other Nebraska farmers, ranchers, and businessman and 2009 candidate for governor David R. Nabity calls: "Nebraska . . . the good life."

Chapter Three

At Home in Nebraska

Driving through Nebraska, some travelers question why people live on such barren land. In the 1980s a national television interviewer asked a traveler where to find Ainsworth, the place where he was going for a horseshoe tournament. The man replied that Ainsworth was "in the middle of nowhere."

Even some folks who live in the state joke about its wide-open spaces and faraway towns. But many more Nebraskans are proud of their roots and what their state offers. Ainsworth residents responded to the interview with the traditional Nebraska can-do spirit. Town leaders now hold an annual Middle of Nowhere Celebration. Ainsworth also declared itself Nebraska's Country Music Capital, with its own theme song praising the town—a 1997 festival winner called "In the Middle of Nowhere."

A librarian from Lincoln sums up the feelings of many about their state. "I could never leave," she says. "Everything we need is right here."

FINDING A PLACE TO LIVE

Over the centuries diverse peoples have made Nebraska their home. Among the earliest were the Pawnee, Oto, Missouri, Omaha, and Ponca

Nebraskans are proud of their heritage and what their state has to offer.

Indians. Later, Winnebago, Lakota, Cheyenne, and others joined them. Today, approximately 17,000 American Indians live in Nebraska. More than four thousand live on the Omaha, Ponca, Winnebago, and Santee Sioux reservations in the northeast. Thurston County contains the Omaha and Winnebago reservations, which give the region's population an American-Indian majority.

Over the years Nebraska has become home to a diverse population.

Ninety-two percent of Nebraska's population is of white European heritage. The first large group of European settlers that came to Nebraska in the nineteenth century was German. Railroad companies and state immigration agents advertised in Europe that land was free in the American West. Czech, Swedish, Danish, Russian, and Irish immigrants followed the Germans.

In the late nineteenth and early twentieth centuries Latinos migrated to Nebraska. They came mainly to work in sugar beet fields or in meatpacking companies. In recent years people from Vietnam, Cambodia, the Middle East, and Central America have left their strife-ridden nations for a chance to build a new life in America. Many moved to Lincoln. "We have very active religious communities who work hard to sponsor refugees," says Lincoln resident Josie Sheffield. Citizens donate everything the newcomers need to get started. Several organizations help them find jobs, schools, and permanent homes. As newsman Brad Penner reported, "They'll find a helping hand in Nebraska."

Today, Nebraskans of German ancestry comprise the largest ethnic group in the state. They settled throughout Nebraska but especially in its eastern counties. The nation's largest Czech population lives in Nebraska. Butler County boasts one of only two counties in the United States with a majority of Czech Americans.

New foreign-born residents comprise the biggest increase in Nebraska's population. By some estimates the number of foreign-born workers moving to Nebraska has increased 5.5 percent since the 1990s. As elsewhere in the United States, the greatest number of foreign-born families come from Mexico and Latin America. Hispanic residents comprise about 7.5 percent of Nebraska's population.

Dressed in traditional German costume, these singers entertain at the Central Nebraska Ethnic Festival in downtown Grand Island.

ETHNIC NEBRASKA

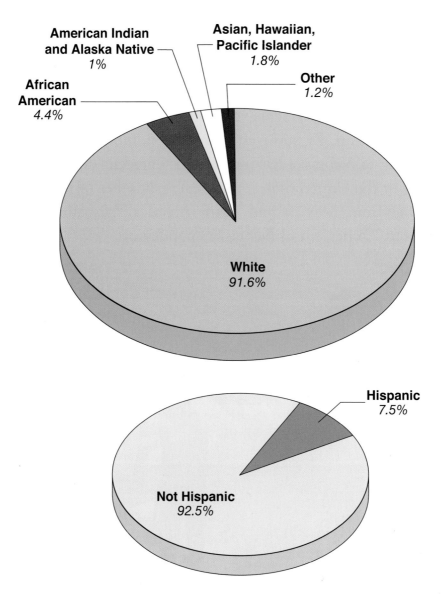

American Indian
and Alaska Native
1%

Asian, Hawaiian,
Pacific Islander
1.8%

African
American
4.4%

Other
1.2%

White
91.6%

Hispanic
7.5%

Not Hispanic
92.5%

Note: A person of Cuban, Mexican, Puerto Rican, South or Central American,
or other Spanish culture or origin, regardless of race, is defined as Hispanic.

AFRICAN-AMERICAN MIGRATION NORTH

The promise of opportunity lured people from other regions of the United States. African-American families, which now comprise about 4.4 percent of Nebraska's population, moved to the state after the Civil War. They were attracted by the opportunities to find jobs in the cities or to claim land. Some who followed the Underground Railroad northward stayed. They farmed, joined the military, and fought in World War II.

North Omaha has long been the location of a thriving community of African Americans.

After the war African Americans in Nebraska battled for equal rights, as did those in other states. In 1938 Mildred Brown had started the *Omaha Star*, a newspaper devoted to issues of racial equality in the African-American community. The Lincoln Urban League, a group of blacks, organized demonstrations to integrate housing, sport centers, and restaurants. During the 1950s and 1960s league members and other civil rights organizations pushed for equality in schools and job opportunities.

Omaha-born Malcolm X became a well-known national civil rights activist. He preached equal rights for all African Americans. Born Malcolm Little, he chose the X to show that he rejected the slave name given to his ancestors. Malcolm X became an outspoken leader in the Nation of Islam, a black religious and political organization. Other members of this group who disagreed with his views shot and killed him on February 27, 1965, in New York City.

CITY FOLKS

With an estimated 1,774,571 residents in 2007, Nebraska ranks thirty-eighth in population among the states. Close to half of the population lives in two large cities in eastern Nebraska: Lincoln and Omaha. Both are growing rapidly. Downtown Omaha, with an estimated 430,000 people in 2005, bursts with new high-rise office complexes, while older portions of the city are being renovated. Cultural organizations are thriving. Attendance is increasing at ethnic sites such as El Museo Latino and Great Plains Black Museum.

Lincoln, the state capital, is stretching its boundaries, with about 249,000 people in 2005. New neighborhoods are appearing, providing

The Old Market Historic District in downtown Omaha is a favorite gathering spot among city folk.

homes for incoming families. "The suburbs are growing so fast," says one retiree. "It used to be that our young people would grow up in Lincoln and hardly wait to leave. But now they get out to L.A. or Dallas and look around, and think, Lincoln doesn't seem so bad after all!"

COUNTRY FOLKS

While some Nebraskans live in sizable cities, many prefer life in small towns or rural areas. "It's the best life there is," insists Panhandle rancher Lil Morava. "Even though in dry years it's bitter, I would never trade it for living down in Scottsbluff."

Almost 90 percent of Nebraskans live in cities and towns with fewer than three thousand people. The state boasts hundreds of towns with less than one thousand residents. Small towns allow folks to spread out and enjoy the land. Only about twenty-three people occupy each square mile of land in Nebraska.

In eastern Nebraska towns and farms are not far from each other. But in western Nebraska roads continue for miles without a town, house, or driveway in sight. "Look at the addresses by the driveways when you go out west," advises a Nebraska City native. "No street names; they just mark the township, range, and section numbers." But whether people have next-door neighbors or live 20 miles from the nearest ranch, a community feeling exists. People are friendly.

"That's why we live here," says Heather Kreifel of Nebraska City. "We moved down from Columbus. Here, the town is small enough that everyone knows who you are, and no one is in such a hurry that they honk their horn at you if you don't take a right turn at a red light." Indeed, rural Nebraskans know their road manners. On long, flat stretches of open road, drivers passing each another nearly always wave as if to say "Hello, fellow traveler!"

There are downsides to small-town life, however. Some people prefer the greater range of activity available in larger cities. Big cities also offer the greatest employment opportunities and broader choices of goods and services. The result has been a loss of young people from rural Nebraska. As young people mature, many abandon rural areas for bigger cities, leaving an older population behind. Town leaders often find they must consolidate city services, such as health care and schools, in order to afford them.

Many Nebraskans prefer life in small towns, such as Maxwell with an estimated population of 320 people.

POPULATION DENSITY

Persons per square mile

0.0 to 0.9	1 to 6.9	7 to 79.9	80 to 159.9	160 to 299.9	300 to 2,999.9	3,000 to 66,940

While content with her western Nebraska roots, student Addy Raymer confesses, "There are pluses and minuses to living out here. The scenery is beautiful and the wildlife and recreation is more than people think it is. But even though people pull together and try to help, if there is an emergency, it's difficult to get trained medics quickly. There are a lot of agricultural accidents, and it takes a long time to airlift someone to Rapid City or Denver."

READING AND WRITING

Nebraskans pride themselves on their good education system. The University of Nebraska in Lincoln is the state's flagship university, and it is known for many firsts. To name just a few, the university started the first advanced doctorate program west of the Mississippi River and the world's first undergraduate psychology lab and ecology studies programs.

Education is a high priority for Nebraskans.

Local public and parochial schools provide solid elementary and high school education. But lower enrollment in rural areas has forced some school districts to merge in order to cut costs. This limits the number of extracurricular activities a district can offer, as money goes to busing students longer distances and to other expenses.

One hot-button issue for Nebraska education involves funding. As in several other states, local property taxes provide the largest share of education funding. This sometimes creates unequal education systems. Areas with a large property tax base from expensive homes and businesses glean the most taxes. This results in more money to fund a variety of school programs. In poorer areas, however, fewer property taxes generate revenue for schools. Children in poorer areas often go without after-school sports, advanced high school courses, and early childhood programs because their districts lack funding. They also attend schools with larger class sizes.

CELEBRATING HOLIDAYS

"The spirit of a people lives in its history" is engraved on the wall of the Nebraska State Historical Society headquarters in Lincoln. Nebraskans love to celebrate their heritage. Local festivals celebrate the people who settled Nebraska's regions and what they've accomplished.

On March 4, 2008, the Thurston County Board of Supervisors enacted a law granting a paid holiday to all county employees for Native American Day, a holiday that falls on the fourth Monday of September. The holiday was already a special day without being a paid holiday. "This is our step in trying to recognize American-Indian contributions to our society in the United States," board member Darren Wolfe told a *Journal Star* reporter.

American Indians claim their own holiday in the form of a powwow. The Winnebago Powwow provides an opportunity for the Ho-Chunk, or Winnebago, Nation to gather for traditional dances and music. The powwow honors their last war chief, Little Priest. Little Priest died in 1866 of wounds he received while serving in the U.S. Army.

American Indians dance in traditional tribal costume at the Winnebago Powwow.

NEBRASKAN POWWOW

The oldest ongoing celebration in Nebraska is a powwow on the Omaha reservation called *Umonhon*, meaning "Omaha": Harvest Hethushka. Powwows celebrate American-Indian culture with dance, music, chants, food, and traditional crafts. During the main event, people gather around a large circle to watch dancers perform. The dancers wear costumes decorated with beads and feathers, which have been passed from generation to generation. The music is also handed down. One year Omaha songs recorded more than a century ago were played for the crowd. Many Omahans said, "I know that song; we still sing that song!" Another important part of the powwow is the "giveaway." During this ceremony the hosts honor their guests by offering them gifts, usually blankets or food baskets. American Indians have a strong sense of generosity, and a giveaway often lasts quite a while!

Another favorite holiday is Arbor Day. Nebraska City resident J. Sterling Morton, editor of Nebraska's first newspaper, proposed the holiday in 1872. After moving from Detroit, Michigan, in 1854, Morton noticed that the lack of trees kept settlers from staying in Nevada. He suggested a tree-planting day to remedy the situation. During the first Arbor Day celebration two years later Nebraskans planted more than one million trees. Lawmakers in other states liked the idea. They chose

Morton's birthday, April 22, as the day to celebrate trees. Today, trees are shipped from Nebraska City to every state that participates in the tree-planting holiday.

Tree planting didn't just happen on private land. In 1902 President Theodore Roosevelt established the Nebraska National Forest. In the desertlike Sandhills, people hand-planted 13 million seedlings. Nebraska houses the only planted forest in the National Forest System and today provides seedlings to other National Forest lands that have been burned or logged.

Morton's farm in Nebraska City now houses the National Arbor Day Foundation. On Arbor Day people flock to the town to enjoy barbecues, music, and environmental exhibits, and of course to plant trees. "I packaged up eight hundred seedlings myself this year," says one Nebraska City businesswoman. "We're expecting a lot of kids; this is our biggest event."

Just about every little town boasts some unique celebration that relives the old days. The Blue Sky Jubilee in the small farming community of Anselmo has turtle and bicycle races, square dances, and even a greased pig contest. Sheep farmer Kim Lucas says, "They grease a pig and set it loose with the kids. But most of the kids wind up falling on each other and the pig goes scot free!"

The American cowboy is celebrated each October in Valentine. Poets, musicians, and storytellers recall life on the range, while modern-day ranchers exhibit their talents from long ago. Rumela holds an annual Harvest Festival each August.

Other festivals that honor Nebraska's past include Oregon Trail Days in Scottsbluff and Gering, Fur Trade Days in Chadron, and Wild West rodeos near Buffalo Bill's ranch in North Platte. At county fairs people enjoy watching antique-tractor pulls and reenactments of pioneer life. Ethnic celebrations are also popular. Drive into the farming town of Lexington and you will see billboards that announce "Lexington—an All American City." However, shop signs are written in English and Spanish. Many Latinos moved to Lexington to

Young dancers kick off the annual Czech Festival in Wilber, Nebraska.

work in the large meatpacking plant that opened in 1990. Now the growing city is nearly one-quarter Latino. Each May Lexington celebrates its ethnic heritage with Latin dancing and Mexican music at a Cinco de Mayo festival. Each summer Wilber, the self-proclaimed Czech Capital of the United States, holds the Wilber Czech Festival. Churches and organizations offer traditional ethnic foods, such as dumplings, roast duck, kraut (cabbage), rye bread, and *kolache* (jam-filled pastries). But the real treats are the activities: the town crowns Miss Czech-Slovak USA; the Wilber Museum offers Czech heritage demonstrations; and there is a parade, Czech dancing, and an accordion show. Other fun-filled ethnic festivals are the Greek Festival in Bridgeport, the St. Patrick's Day celebration in O'Neill, and the Danish celebration of Grundlovsfest in Dannebrog.

Pretzels had a long European history before traveling with German immigrants to the United States. According to legend, pretzels first appeared in 610 CE in southern France or northern Italy. Monks formed three holes from strips of dough to represent the Christian Trinity. Travelers brought the *pretiola*, meaning "little reward," to Austria and Germany. In Frankfurt, Germany, merchants renamed the twisted dough *bretzel*, or pretzel. Each fall, visitors to Oktoberfest in Omaha often snack on soft German pretzels.

1 tablespoon yeast dissolved in 1 cup warm water
3 tablespoons brown sugar
2 teaspoons salt
3 1/2 cups flour
2 teaspoons baking soda dissolved in 1 cup hot water
1 egg beaten in 1 teaspoon water
coarse salt, sesame seeds, or cinnamon sugar

Mix yeast water, brown sugar, and salt in a large mixing bowl. Add flour and stir until a smooth dough forms. If too sticky, add flour to mold. Divide dough into six (for large pretzels) or twelve (for small pretzels) pieces. Roll each dough portion into a thin rope about the length of a pencil. Form dough into pretzel shape, and pinch ends together. Place on a greased cookie sheet. Let pretzels rise until their size doubles (about one hour). Dip each pretzel into the baking soda and water mixture. Brush with the egg and water mixture. Sprinkle with coarse salt, sesame seeds, or cinnamon sugar. Bake at 450 ºF for twelve to fifteen minutes or until browned.

FAVORITE ACTIVITIES

College football brings Nebraskans of every ethnic group together. It is hard to be in Nebraska and not know when it is game day. This is the day the University of Nebraska Cornhuskers play football. "Cornhusker football is huge here," says Diane Thomas. "Everyone lives to go to games from the end of August to the last goal time. Lincoln turns into the biggest city in the state because of the games."

On game day spectators outfitted in the school colors of red and white engulf Lincoln. Across Nebraska and beyond, Cornhusker fans are enthusiastic. Whether seated in the stadium or watching the game on television, Nebraskans all join together on game day to cheer, "Go, Big Red!"

"When I taught school, whoever the Cornhuskers played that week became the subject of projects about other states," Thomas remembers. "Kids loved it. They went out of their way to prepare great papers."

Outdoor sports provide other favorite activities. Ask a Nebraskan "What do you like to do here?" and most people will say something to do with the outdoors. Nebraskans love

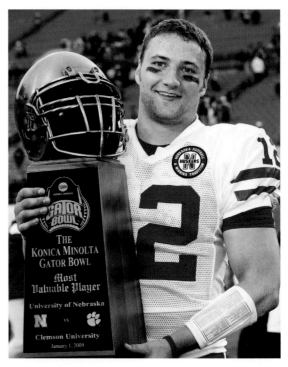

College football is a favorite sport in Nebraska. Here, quarterback Joe Ganz accepts the Nebraska Cornhuskers MVP award in 2009.

to fish, hunt, cycle, and sail. Even in the land once called the Great American Desert, boating remains a favorite sport. A surprising number of driveways display a boat and trailer ready to ply the waters of giant Lake McConaughy or any of the hundreds of other lakes and reservoirs in the state. Canoeists and kayakers like the 11,000 miles of Nebraska rivers and streams. Troy Nutter of the Sandhills says with a smile, "I love the Dismal River; it's so remote, you can get in a canoe and go five or six hours and never see anybody else." Innkeeper Jeanne Goetzinger agrees that the Nebraska landscape is special. Mountain bikers and hunters come from all over the United States to stay in her small hotel in Chadron, near the Pine Ridge. She says, "When I get in the hills, I know I am alive—it's a privilege to be here."

Chapter Four

Equality Before the Law

Nebraska's state motto is "Equality Before the Law." The motto is more than words—it guides how Nebraskans live. Throughout the state's history, lawmakers have valued a sense of fairness in Nebraska government.

INSIDE GOVERNMENT

During territorial days the Platte River divided Nebraskans politically into North Platters and South Platters. Omaha in the north became the territorial capital. South Platters were so unhappy, they threatened to secede and become citizens of Kansas. The battle between South and North Platters continued until Nebraska became the thirty-seventh state in 1867. A committee composed of the first governor, auditor, and secretary of state chose a small village south of the Platte and renamed it Lincoln. The state government remains in Lincoln today and has three branches: executive, legislative, and judicial.

The Nebraska State Capitol, located in Lincoln, is one of the most distinctive statehouses in the United States. Its 400-foot-high tower holds government offices, and visitors can tour its 440-foot-wide base.

Executive

The executive branch has six offices. The governor, lieutenant governor, secretary of state, state treasurer, auditor of public accounts, and attorney general are each elected for four-year terms. The governor, who is head of state, prepares the yearly budget and either signs bills into law or rejects them with a veto. The lieutenant governor acts as president of the legislature and assistant to the governor. If the governor is unable to serve, the lieutenant governor acts as governor.

Legislative

Nebraska has a legislature unique among the fifty states. The federal government and every state in the nation except Nebraska maintain a legislature with two houses of government, usually a house of representatives and a senate. Nebraska has only one house. This system is called a unicameral legislature, or Unicam. With this system, voters select forty-nine members, called senators, to serve four-year terms. Each senator comes from one of forty-nine districts within the state, each representing approximately 32,200 citizens. Senators are assigned to serve on fourteen different committees that hold public hearings and gather information and opinions on various bills the senators are considering.

In 1934 Nebraskans adopted this one-house system without political parties, such as Democrat, Republican, or Independent. Lawmakers believed the system would make government less complicated and more efficient. Nebraska statesman George William Norris supported the "Nebraska experiment" in the 1930s. He argued that the only reason states had two houses was because they copied the British system. In Britain the king or queen appointed lawmakers to the House of

Dave Heineman won his first full term as governor in 2006 with a historic number of votes.

Lords, and the people voted for lawmakers to serve in the other house of government, the House of Commons. Senator Norris argued that such a system was unnecessary in the United States. He explained, "The Constitutions of our various states are built upon the idea that there is but one class. If this be true, there is no sense or reason in having the same thing done twice, especially if it is to be done by two bodies of men elected in the same way and having the same jurisdiction."

George William Norris represented Nebraska in the U.S. Senate from 1913 to 1943.

The unicameral legislature works very well for Nebraska. Because fewer members of the legislature meet for shorter sessions, Unicam saves Nebraska taxpayers money. Unicam politics supports a spirit of cooperation among senators. Since senators do not run as members of political parties, they have no party to influence their activity. Senators make their own decisions and work with a variety of other legislators.

Judicial

The court system consists of a supreme court, a court of appeals, and district and county courts. Judges serve two-year terms. The supreme court includes a chief justice and six associate justices. The governor appoints them from a list recommended by a legal committee. While the chief justice can come from anywhere in the state, each of the other six judges must represent one of six districts. Together, they hear cases that involve challenges to the state constitution, life imprisonment, or the death penalty. Justices also supervise lawyers practicing in the state and guard against mistakes occurring in the other courts. The court of appeals consists of six judges appointed by the governor.

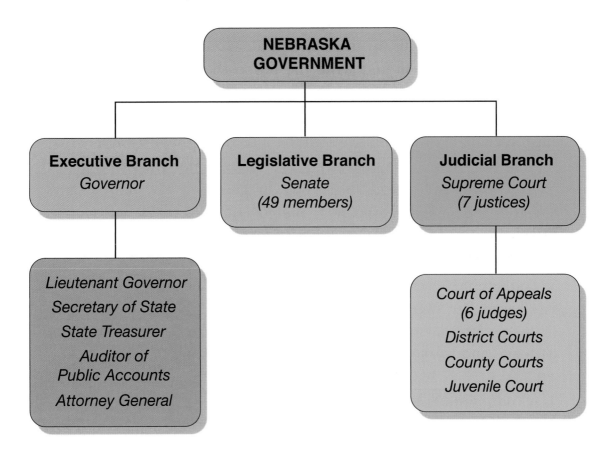

Twelve district courts hear serious cases, such as assaults, that are not heard by the supreme court. Minor cases, such as traffic tickets, are heard in the twelve county courts. If someone disagrees with a district or county court's ruling, that person can request a review by the court of appeals. Sometimes cases are appealed again and are heard by the supreme court.

CREATING LAWS

In Nebraska ideas for laws may come from citizens, special-interest groups, state agencies, or the governor. Nebraska is one of twenty-four states that allow citizens to suggest laws to legislators. The legislator sends the suggestion to the appropriate committee for members to gather information and write the proposed bill. After committee members debate the proposal, they send their recommendation to the full legislature for consideration by all the senators. Some senators may suggest changes or amendments to the bill. If the majority agrees that the bill has merit, senators debate and vote on the bill again. If the majority votes for the bill, it goes to the governor. The bill becomes law after the governor signs it. If the governor rejects the bill, it can still become law if thirty of the forty-nine senators agree to override the governor's veto.

Sometimes even the best laws must be revised. In July 2008 the safe-haven law went into effect. This allowed parents or guardians to leave children up to age eighteen at hospitals or police stations without question if they could not provide for them for any reason. All other states have a similar law. But those states apply the law only to infants, although some cover babies up to one year old.

NEBRASKA
BY COUNTY

By November 2008 thirty-five older children had been left for safe haven at Nebraska hospitals, some of whom were from other states. Parents of troubled teenagers claimed that the state lacked resources to help them. Nebraskans were shocked at the abuse of the law. In fall 2008 Governor Dave Heineman called the legislature into a special session. Lawmakers quickly changed the law to limit safe haven only to infants up to one month old.

POLITICAL DIVIDE

While political parties may not divide Nebraska voters, geography does. Needs are very different for people in opposite ends of the state. "All the power is in Omaha," says a western Nebraska shopkeeper. For the most part, that is true. Most voters live in the east. The most money is generated and transferred there. As a matter of fact, one of the richest men in the entire world, Warren Buffett, controls his corporate empire from an office in Omaha. Buffett began his financial career as a newspaper boy in Omaha at age thirteen. After college in 1965 he took control of the Omaha textile firm Berkshire Hathaway. Always smart, he expanded the company by investing in other industries. He bought into industries involving insurance (Geico), utilities (MidAmerican Energy), food (See's Candies and Dairy Queen), jewelry (Borsheim's), and beverages (Coca-Cola and Anheuser-Busch). Buffett's businesses contributed to an imbalance of wealth and population that put the western part of the state at an economic disadvantage.

One major issue dividing east and west is land. All land in Nebraska is taxed under similar laws. But because a western rancher needs to own more land to earn a living than does an eastern farmer or a city dweller, the rancher pays more in taxes. The legislature is working on this complicated problem. The problem was magnified after state property taxes increased 5.7 percent from 2006 to 2007. Some districts received a 12-percent increase, while others paid 2.1 percent more. Nebraska property owners pay taxes to local and state governments, causing Nebraska taxpayers to pay the seventeenth-highest real estate taxes in the nation. Such high taxes drain family incomes.

But people in the west don't expect relief anytime soon. "Out here in the Panhandle, people talk about seceding and becoming part of Wyoming. We have a lot more in common with Cheyenne than Omaha," laments one resident.

Chapter Five

Nebraskans at Work

Even when the national economy slows to a crawl, Nebraska continues to prosper. Location, laws that support farming and corporations, and a talented and eager workforce keep agriculture, business, and manufacturing strong.

Eastern Nebraska cities are booming. The unemployment rate there remains one of the lowest in the country. Homes cost less than those in other urban areas. Pollution is low compared with other major cities. And with plentiful jobs and good schools and highways, people keep moving to cities such as Omaha and Lincoln.

MANUFACTURING AND BUSINESS

During the past few years Nebraska has attracted several large corporate headquarters, adding jobs and income to the state economy. State laws offer lower taxes to businesses that bring new jobs and investment into Nebraska. Even weather has been a boon to business for companies that prefer to settle in a central state without threats of hurricanes, floods, or earthquakes, such as those that occur on either coast. Omaha, with its

Nebraska farmers regularly produce over one billion bushels of high quality corn.

Irrigated corn in Nebraska is harvested by farm machinery.

large workforce, has especially benefited from corporate and manufacturing growth. Besides being close to Eppley Airfield, Omaha's central location off interstates 80 and 29 allows an easy one-day drive to most major cities in the nation to distribute goods.

Agriculture-related products lead the state's manufacturing economy. These include food processing and the manufacture of fertilizers, farm machinery, and irrigation equipment. Omaha-based ConAgra Foods is the gigantic umbrella group for popular food brands that make everything from prepared meals and soup to popcorn and pork and beans. Union Pacific Railroad and Burlington-Northern/ Santa Fe transport these and other food products, such as Nebraska beef, cattle feed, cereals, and frozen vegetables, nationwide—to local stores and to ports for export.

Over the past few decades Nebraska has worked to diversify its economy. The largest growth has been in service industries. Health care, insurance, and financial services, such as billing and credit card services, saw the greatest expansion, in addition to university, military, and government jobs. Omaha is the headquarters of Mutual of Omaha, a health insurance company that is one of the state's largest employers. Billionaire Warren Buffett of Omaha created Berkshire Hathaway, an umbrella company that holds large stakes in many major companies. He played a key role in buying stakes in companies hurt by the nation's 2008 economic crisis. He is so respected in the financial community that President Barack Obama asked him for advice regularly during his campaign and early presidency.

NEBRASKA WORKFORCE

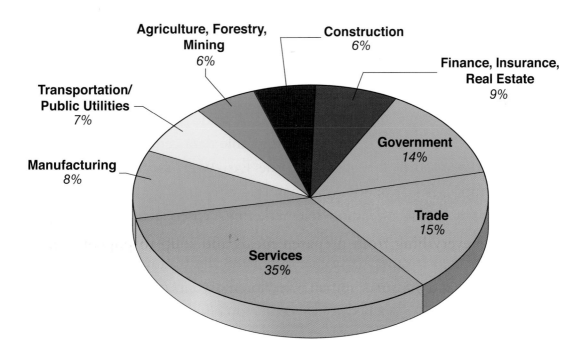

Omaha's legacy of excellence in telecommunications is a result of the presence of the U.S. Strategic Air Command.

Another growth industry involves telecommunications. This industry developed as an outgrowth of activities from the U.S. Strategic Air Command housed in Nebraska. Technology advances made during the 1960s exploded into private businesses by the 1990s. So many telecommunications businesses opened in Omaha that the city became known as the 1-800 Capital of the World. A leader in the field has been MCI WorldCom, which opened a major cable data center in Omaha in 1995. "We wanted to be located on the East-West backbone for cable in the country," MCI's Sandy Steckman told a reporter.

Nebraska is also a leading telemarketing center. Telemarketers are workers who contact people either to sell them things or to poll their opinion for their business customers. In 1988 the Gallup Organization, which studies and measures human behavior, moved its national call center to Lincoln and later opened a call center in Holdrege in south-central Nebraska. The centers hire workers to call people nationwide about topics ranging from food and cleaning-product preferences to politics.

Thanksgiving is the main time to sell turkeys. But in 1953, the C. A. Swanson & Sons Company of Omaha, had a lot of leftover turkey—500,000 pounds of it. That was more than the warehouse could hold, so the meat sat in refrigerated railroad cars and crisscrossed the country. Swanson executives wondered what to do with the extra fowl. That's when a Swanson employee, Gerry Thomas (below), devised a revolutionary idea. He remembered seeing metal serving trays on an airline, so he and a chef prepared a turkey dinner on an aluminum tray and quickly froze the food. Thomas called his idea Swanson's TV Dinners. The idea led to an entire new industry and changed the way many U.S. families ate.

At first no one thought the idea would amount to much. The company believed people wanted home-cooked meals. They questioned whether people watched television at dinnertime. Store managers didn't think much of the TV dinner idea either, but they thought homemakers would buy them anyway in order to reuse the metal trays for storing buttons and other small items. But Thomas proved everybody wrong. By the end of 1953 C. A. Swanson & Sons had sold 10 million Swanson's TV Dinners and revolutionized the food industry. In 1997 an executive with the company declared, "They're part of American culture." A representation of Gerry Thomas's inventive solution to leftover turkey is on display in the Smithsonian Institution in Washington, D.C.

AGRICULTURE

Agriculture and related processing and production of agricultural products remain the most important parts of the state's economy. Indeed, soil is easily Nebraska's greatest natural resource. The state ranks second in U.S. exports of cattle and cattle products, third in feed grains such as corn, and sixth in soybeans and sunflower seeds and oils. Nebraska's hardworking farmers also produce other grains, sorghum, sugar beets, and dry beans worth billions of dollars.

2007 GROSS STATE PRODUCT: $80 Million

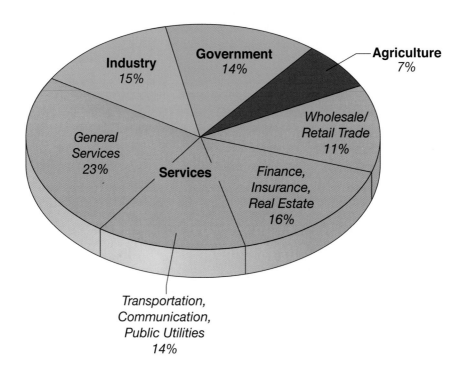

Industry 15%

Government 14%

Agriculture 7%

General Services 23%

Services

Wholesale/ Retail Trade 11%

Finance, Insurance, Real Estate 16%

Transportation, Communication, Public Utilities 14%

But with its constant uncertainties, farming is a difficult life, and it's always changing. "Family farms are bigger now. There's less manpower and more machinery," says Sidney city manager Gary Person.

The Nebraska legislature has worked hard to help farmers stay afloat. During the 1980s, a generally bad economy, crop prices declined, and many farmers could no longer pay their bills. Large corporations started buying up family farms and ranches, which threatened local communities. Lawmakers passed Initiative 300 in 1982 to block giant nonfarm corporations outside Nebraska from buying state farms or ranches. The law helped preserve small farms, but it had opponents from the beginning. Investors wanted to purchase land without government interference. Some ranchers found it more difficult to sell their land. In 2008 a judge declared the law unconstitutional. But the debate continues, with legislators devising amendments that pass court approval.

"We will be back," Dan Owens of the Center for Rural Affairs told a reporter. "Nebraskans understand the importance of family farms and ranches, as well as corporate responsibility."

Among the main concerns of cattle ranchers is making sure that livestock have adequate food and water. The high-plains grasses are rich in nutrients, so ranchers do not give cattle extra feed. But they need to share the rangeland fairly. "There's a lot of peer pressure around here to not overgraze the land," says Ruthann Knudsen, who lives in the Panhandle. "Cows make it or they don't."

Nebraska has been a leader in using irrigation in agriculture. Ranchers and farmers in dry-land areas benefit from the enormous Oglala Aquifer. Windmills and irrigation wells dot the landscape, pumping water for livestock. But many people are concerned that more water has been drawn in the last decade than ever before. Knudsen supports her neighbors, however. "I think the ranchers out here are pretty good resource managers," she says. "They conserve the land and treat it with respect."

Nebraska cattle ranchers make sure their livestock have abundant water and food.

EARNING A LIVING

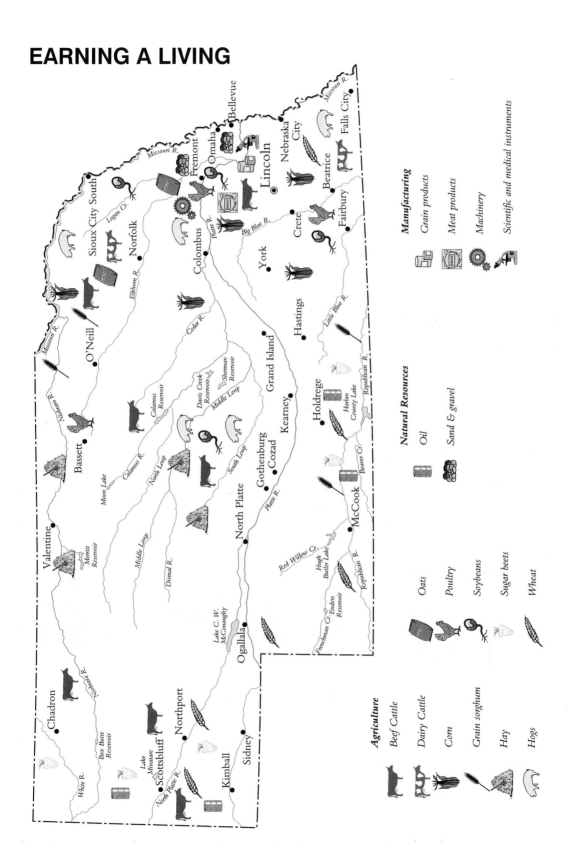

Manufacturing

Grain products

Meat products

Machinery

Scientific and medical instruments

Natural Resources

Oil

Sand & gravel

Agriculture

Beef Cattle

Dairy Cattle

Corn

Grain sorghum

Hay

Hogs

Oats

Poultry

Soybeans

Sugar beets

Wheat

NATURAL RESOURCES

A small amount, less than one percent, of Nebraska income comes from mining. Portland cement, clay, sand and gravel, and cement and lime fuel construction industries. These natural resources go into producing concrete, bricks, and other building materials. Coal, oil, and uranium mined in western Nebraska also contribute to the state's economy.

Nebraska plays an increasingly important role in helping the nation pursue clean energy resources. Nebraska has become a leader in the production of biofuels, such as ethanol and soy diesel. Numerous plants process crops into fuel. The American Wind Energy Association ranks Nebraska the sixth-leading state in capabilities to turn wind power into electricity. So far, the industry is testing these capabilities.

Nebraska's Kimball wind farm produces enough electricity to power two thousand homes annually.

The Sandhills of north-central Nebraska and the high plains of the Panhandle have sprouted several 230-feet-tall steel windmills, or wind turbines. The first turbines appeared in Springview in 1999. They generated enough electricity to power about four hundred homes. Residents were so pleased, they began an annual Turbine Days celebration and renamed the main street Turbine Avenue. By 2007 investors built wind turbines near Lincoln, Omaha, Kimball, and Ainsworth. The state contained forty-six wind turbines that produced enough electricity to power about 21,500 homes, or one percent of the state's electricity need. Plans continue to harness clean, free wind to fulfill 10 percent of the state's energy needs by 2020.

Chapter Six

The Open Road

Interstate 80 is one of the country's busiest east-west highways, and it slices border to border across Nebraska. But traveling on it won't really let you see much of the state. According to Omaha native Jim Royer, "You gotta get off the interstate if you want to see anything."

BIG-CITY VARIETY

Before leaving the highway, visitors to Nebraska need to explore Omaha, the state's largest city. With 433,000 people, Omaha is the nation's forty-second-largest city. The city grew from a transportation and meatpacking hub to an important location for industry and insurance companies. Omaha prides itself on preserving historic buildings and old ethnic neighborhoods. The historic Old Market district displays local and foreign products in unusual shops, bookstores, and restaurants.

Yet, Omaha boasts a variety of skyscrapers and modern cultural events. The city's Henry Doorly Zoo houses a swing bridge over the world's largest indoor rain forest in addition to maintaining the Scott Aquarium,

Omaha, the largest city in the state of Nebraska, is nestled along the Missouri River.

with an 850,000-gallon fish tank. The Joslyn Art Museum, an extension of Washington D.C.'s Smithsonian Institution, displays artwork by famed painters Claude Monet and Jackson Pollock, and by glass artist Dale Chihuly. For entertainment the Holland Center for Performing Arts features the Omaha Symphony. The Omaha Community Playhouse offers plays at the nation's largest community theater. And Qwest Center Omaha hosts popular music performances.

Omaha's Henry Doorly Zoo features the rainforests of Asia, Africa, and South America.

TEN LARGEST CITIES

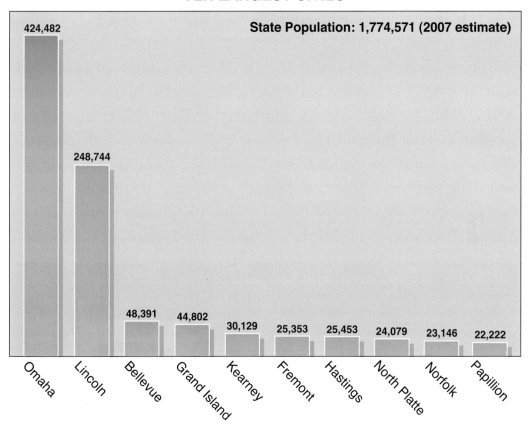

State Population: 1,774,571 (2007 estimate)

424,482 — Omaha
248,744 — Lincoln
48,391 — Bellevue
44,802 — Grand Island
30,129 — Kearney
25,353 — Fremont
25,453 — Hastings
24,079 — North Platte
23,146 — Norfolk
22,222 — Papillion

RIVER JOURNEYS

The earliest and easiest way to travel to Nebraska was by water. Today, river roads lead travelers to some of Nebraska's most historic sites. Nebraska City is an interesting town along the Missouri River. It is home to the stately Arbor Lodge, the residence of Arbor Day's founder, J. Sterling Morton. The Morton estate now sponsors the National Arbor Day Foundation, which manages the Arbor Day Farm. The farm hosts various tree-related activities, including climbing 50 feet to a tree house, building with wooden blocks, and leaving with a free seedling to plant at home.

The town is also the site of Allen B. Mayhew's simple pioneer cabin, built in 1855. He constructed a root cellar nearby. Mayhew's brother-in-law, John H. Kagi, was an antislavery activist and an associate of abolitionist John Brown. Over the years legends spread that the Mayhew cabin was a station on the Underground Railroad. Although the cabin and root cellar were once known as John Brown's Cave, there is no evidence that John Brown ever visited the cabin. John Kagi once brought several African Americans to the Mayhew cabin for breakfast. Kagi's connection

Built in 1855 and restored in 2005, Allen Mayhew's pioneer cabin still stands for visitors to see.

to the cabin and suggestions that it may have sheltered escaping slaves made the cabin a popular tourist attraction. The tiny home is still furnished as it was in Mayhew's time.

No river is more identified with Nebraska than the Platte. This waterway flows past some of the state's foremost attractions. The Great Platte River Road carried many fur traders, gold seekers, Mormons, and settlers west to Oregon, California, and Utah. Reminders of their journey are plentiful today. The Stuhr Museum of the Prairie Pioneer near Grand Island covers the histories of American Indians and Old West adventurers. Original structures, such as a general store, a railroad depot, wooden sidewalks, and a Pawnee earthen lodge, have been moved to or constructed on museum grounds and preserved with great care. The museum looks so authentic that three television movies have been filmed there to date, including *Sarah, Plain and Tall*, Patricia MacLachlan's 1986 Newbery Medal–winning story of a frontier girl living on the Great Plains.

Farther along the Great Platte River Road is Fort Kearny, which was built in 1848 to protect pioneers traveling on the Oregon Trail. The fort, now a state historic site, is a good place to relive early American military history. Nearby, springtime bird-watchers come to view migrating sandhill cranes. Those who miss the migration find another wonderful wildlife experience at Elm Creek Wild Horse and Burro Facility. Here, wild horses and burros that have been rounded up from government-owned land are given a home.

Continuing west, the land changes from rolling prairie and farmland to high plains. Near the town of Oglala a dam holds back the North Platte River, forming Lake McConaughy, the state's largest body of water.

Lake McConaughy, the largest man-made reservoir in Nebraska, has become a favorite with swimmers, sailboaters, and many other outdoor fun seekers.

The setting feels removed, but the lake teems with boaters, campers, and outdoor enthusiasts.

Nearby Ash Hollow was a treasured watering hole in the days when mastodons roamed the area. Ancestors of the Apache lived in this sheltered valley, drank the clear water, and enjoyed the shade of ash trees growing in rare abundance. In the mid–nineteenth century overland pioneers passed through. They found Ash Hollow to be something of an oasis during their trek across the plains. Today the site features an interpretive history center and an old schoolhouse set in the whispering quiet of replaced ash groves. A breathtaking view of the surrounding ridges can be seen from the top of Windlass Hill. From this vantage point pioneers confronted a steep descent as their wagons rattled wildly down the hill into Ash Hollow.

Another historic site along the Great Platte River Road past Scottsbluff is Chimney Rock. While pioneers plodded west, they could see this towering rock formation ahead of them for several days. Although travel is faster today, Chimney Rock remains an amazing landmark and has been designated a National Historical Site. Travelers have always stopped to gaze at it and other nearby formations. "I taught fourth grade for twenty-five years," says a retired Kearney schoolteacher, "and I can say Chimney Rock, Courthouse, and Jail Rocks were the best field trips we took. Kids couldn't wait to go."

Many rivers besides the Missouri and Platte crisscross Nebraska. Outdoorspeople follow the Dismal or the Loup through the Sandhills to be surrounded by sandy wilderness. The hilly sand dunes are dotted with rivers, streams, and lakes. Sandhills resident Troy Nutter jokes, "You get eastern Nebraskans out here and they think they are in the mountains."

THE SKY OVERLOAD

"There's no darker dark than in the Sandhills," says resident Troy Nutter. When astronomers want to watch the night sky, the Sandhills are one of the first places they head for. Hundreds of amateur astronomers from as far away as Puerto Rico and China enjoy the Nebraska Star Party each year near Valentine, in the heart of the Sandhills. Star parties are outdoor-observing sessions that are held at remote locations to avoid lights from urban areas. Even small towns generate what is called sky glow. The remote Sandhills give prairie astronomers the opportunity to see an array of stars and galaxies that aren't visible in more populated areas.

Away from light pollution, Nebraska Star partygoers get a fantastic view of the Milky Way, the northern lights, and meteor showers. Another exciting sight for amateur astronomers is the Cat's Eye Nebula. Scientists believe the nebula is an unusual cluster of two dying stars surrounded by a halo of gases. For Nebraska Star partygoers, sights such as these truly make the Nebraska night sky a marvel.

Nutter is not alone in his fondness for Nebraska's wilderness. Each year, tens of thousands of people visit the wild and scenic Niobrara River to canoe, hike, fish, and swim. The Niobrara rushes through six different ecosystems, from grasslands to sandstone canyons; has more than ninety waterfalls; and provides a habitat for herds of deer, elk, and buffalo.

The Niobrara River provides habitat for white-tailed deer.

ANCIENT WONDERS

"I must have slept through history class," says Korinda Licking of Thedford, "because when I went up north to the Ashfall beds, I couldn't believe it!" Ashfall Fossil Beds State Historical Park is a world-renowned

Buried by volcanic ash 10 million years ago, these well preserved rhinoceros skeletons can be viewed at the Ashfall Fossil Beds State Historical Park.

fossil site. The Nebraska grasslands of 10 million years ago were home to an incredibly diverse array of ancient creatures that congregated around watering holes. Far to the west a volcano erupted, spewing a cloud of ash across the land. When the ash fell over this particular watering hole, it suffocated all the animals at once and buried them.

Even in a land noted for fossils, the Ashfall fossil beds are remarkable. Not only is it rare to find whole herds buried together as they are here, but it is also rare that so many different creatures died at once. Remains of prehistoric horses, camels, giant tortoises, and rhinos have all been found at the site. Many skeletons were discovered next to an imprint of the animals' final footsteps or with a last meal of grass in their mouths. Most of the fossils at the site are still buried, but scientists continue to carefully uncover the bones. They believe that large meat eaters hunted in the area, so they hope to uncover a saber-toothed tiger or a bear-dog someday.

Travelers who follow the Niobrara River valley west enter the Oglala National Grassland. Ancient rivers long since dried up, wind, and rain helped erode a portion of this landscape to create winding mazes and odd, umbrella-shaped rock formations now known as Toadstool Geologic Park. Scientists and visitors have discovered fossils 30 million years old in the park. These include ancestors of modern dogs, cats, horses, and wild pigs. The area's fossils are of such high quality and abundance that museums around the world exhibit them.

Nebraska's western Panhandle contains some of the wildest and most remote country in the nation. On distant hills cattle wander the range, and windmills spin. Travelers can easily go without seeing a car, tractor, house, or driveway along the lonely stretch of highway from Fort Robinson to the Agate Fossil Beds National Monument. "It's very serene," says Ruthann

Knudsen, superintendent of the monument, "and there is nowhere to get to from here—we are a long way from places."

Driving the lonely road to the Agate fossil beds is well worth it. In the early 1900s the area became popular with East Coast scientists looking for fossils. One interesting creature uncovered was *Palaeocastor*, a beaverlike animal that dug burrows in corkscrew patterns. A hike on Devil's Corkscrew Trail offers views of squirrely prehistoric tunnels firsthand. Remains of prehistoric camels and *Moropus*, an animal related to both the rhinoceros and the horse, were also discovered at the site.

The history surrounding the Agate fossil beds is more than just ancient. The Agate Fossil Beds National Monument was once Agate Springs Ranch, which was owned by a frontier couple, James and Kate Cook. The Cooks and Red Cloud, a Lakota chief, became friends. At the time there was much strife between Red Cloud's people and the U.S. military. James Cook often intervened on behalf of the Lakota. To show his gratitude and to ensure that some part of the Lakota way of life was preserved, Red Cloud presented many gifts to the Cooks. Among them were ceremonial costumes, saddles, war clubs, moccasins, pipes, bows, and painted buffalo hides. The collection, which is on display at the park, presents an astonishing depiction of Plains Indian life.

THE WILD WEST

"The Nebraska Panhandle's motto should be 'We're Not Omaha,'" Ruthann Knudsen says, laughing, "because it's the West out here!" She is right. The Nebraska Panhandle is a land of cattle drives, buffalo herds, historic battlefields, and magnificent Great Plains scenery. Touring this region provides many reasons to admire the rich history and incredible beauty of the American West.

PLACES TO SEE

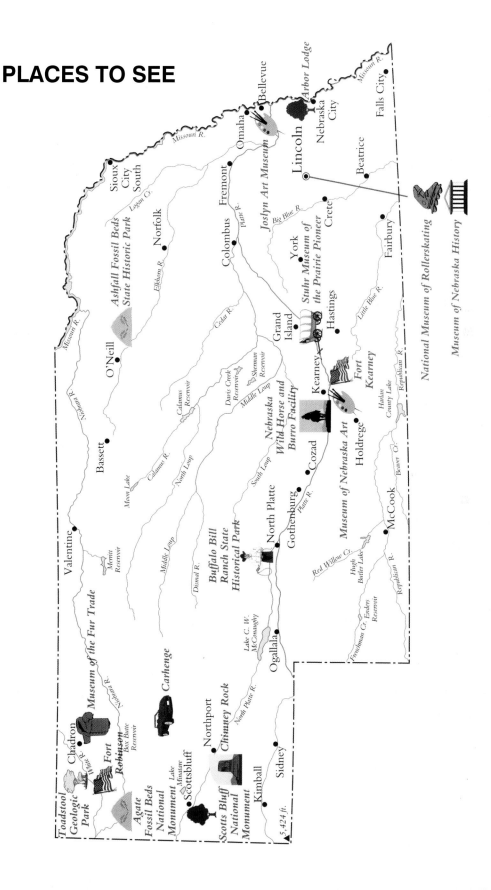

Among the Panhandle's most spectacular sites is Fort Robinson. This fort was built in the 1870s to control the Indians at the nearby Red Cloud Agency. The great Lakota warrior Crazy Horse was killed by a soldier here, and Cheyenne chiefs Dull Knife and Red Cloud were held prisoner on the grounds. The fort was a military outpost into the twentieth century, housing German prisoners during World War II. Today the fort's controversial past stands in stark contrast to its extraordinary beauty. "Fort Rob is awesome!" claims Alliance resident Addy Raymer. "It's past isn't great, but there is just so much to do there that you just try to put your feelings aside." Fort Rob, as it is affectionately called, is located in the Pine Ridge region. Herds of buffalo roam through canyons surrounded by high white cliffs, rugged buttes, and hills covered in deep green pines. The fort occupies Nebraska's most popular state park, where there is plenty to do, from horseback riding and hunting to fishing, cross-country skiing, mountain biking, and hiking.

The Museum of the Fur Trade in tiny Chadron displays history of a different kind. The building holds a phenomenal collection of weapons, beadwork, furs, costumes, and everyday supplies used by trappers, traders, and Indians from 1600 to 1900. "You have to go," insists Chadron resident Jeanne Goetzinger. "There's nothing like it anywhere in the world."

There is also nothing in the world quite like Dobby's Frontier Town in Alliance. Kenneth "Dobby" Lee, who died in 2009, created a town of nineteen renovated buildings. He filled these buildings with historic objects and opened them to the public. Before he retired, he drove a school bus to athletic competitions all over the Great Plains. "I drove everywhere," he says. "We would go places and see stuff and

Fort Robinson, Western Nebraska's premier state park, displays its more than 22,000 acres of exquisite Pine Ridge scenery.

then the next time we went, it'd be gone. That's history going down the drain. That's why I started collecting." Walking around Lee's property takes hours—and not because of its size. The place is crowded with original frontier buildings such as a general store, a courthouse, a jail, a barbershop, the area's first gas station, and the one-room cabin of the first African Americans to homestead in the county. "You should read about Robert Ball-Anderson," says Lee. "He wrote a book called *From Slavery to Affluence* about how he went from being a Civil War veteran and former slave to a homesteader who made it rich in diamonds and real estate. Look, here's a picture of me with his wife, one of the last Civil War widows. She just died a few years back." Visitors can sit in the Andersons' cabin, now in Lee's yard, on old handmade chairs. Amazingly, everything in Frontier Town is out in the open. Visitors can touch, inspect, and explore to their heart's content.

Although Alliance is a small town, it boasts more than one unusual and inviting attraction. Just a couple of miles outside of town, in the middle of wide, flat wheat fields, is a heart-stopping sight that is like no place else in the world. In England a giant four-thousand-year-old stone circle called Stonehenge has long inspired the curious. One such person was Jim Reinders, an Alliance native, who spent several years in England. After he returned to Alliance, Reinders looked at the old cars parked around the family farm. He and his relatives cooked up a scheme to re-create Stonehenge using Cadillacs and Oldsmobiles instead of rocks. It turned into a huge project. They painted all the cars gray and, using cranes and forklifts, stuck them upright in the earth in the same formation as the stones in England. "Carhenge" rises as dramatically above Alliance wheat fields as Stonehenge does above England's Salisbury Plain.

Carhenge, a replica of England's Stonehenge, consists of thirty-eight automobiles arranged in a circle measuring about 96 feet in diameter.

City officials were originally displeased with what they considered an eyesore. But as word got out, tourists came from all over the world to admire Jim Reinders' amusing and monumental tribute. Once city officials realized they had a gem of an attraction on their hands, they sensibly allowed Reinders' vision to remain.

Carhenge is a fine representation of Nebraska and its people—original, hardworking, agreeable, and quietly worldly. Carhenge is another good reason to get to know Nebraska.

THE FLAG: *The state flag was designed in 1925 and officially adopted in 1963. It shows the Nebraska seal in gold and silver in the center of a blue background.*

THE SEAL: *The Nebraska seal shows symbols of the state's history and economy: a worker with a hammer and anvil, a cabin and sheaves of grain, a steamboat traveling up the Missouri River, and a train heading toward the Rocky Mountains. A banner above these scenes displays the state motto: "Equality Before the Law." Surrounding the entire seal are the words "Great Seal of the State of Nebraska" and "March 1, 1867," the date Nebraska entered the Union. The seal was adopted by the state legislature on June 13, 1867.*

State Survey

Statehood: March 1, 1867

Origin of Name: From the Oto/Omaha Indian word *nibrathka*, which means "flat water." It was the tribes' name for Nebraska's main river, the Platte.

Nickname: Cornhusker State

Capital: Lincoln

Motto: Equality Before the Law

Bird: Western meadowlark

Mammal: White-tailed deer

Fish: Channel catfish

Flower: Goldenrod

Grass: Little bluestem

Tree: Cottonwood

Western meadowlark

Goldenrod

BEAUTIFUL NEBRASKA

"Beautiful Nebraska" was adopted as the official state song in 1967.

Insect: Honeybee

Rock: Prairie agate

Gemstone: Blue chalcedony

Fossil: Mammoth

GEOGRAPHY

Highest Point: 5,424 feet above sea level, in Kimball County

Lowest Point: 840 feet above sea level, in Richardson County

Area: 77,358 square miles

Greatest Distance North to South: 206 miles

Greatest Distance East to West: 462 miles

Bordering States: South Dakota to the north, Colorado and Wyoming to the west, Kansas to the south, Iowa and Missouri to the east

Hottest Recorded Temperature: 118 °F at Geneva on July 15, 1934; at Hartington on July 17, 1936; and at Minden on July 24, 1936

Coldest Recorded Temperature: −47 °F at Camp Clarke, near Northport, on February 12, 1899

Average Annual Precipitation: 22 inches

Major Rivers: Big Blue, Elkhorn, Little Blue, Loup, Missouri, Niobrara, North Platte, Platte, Republican, South Platte

Major Lakes: Calamus, Enders, Harlan County, Harry Strunk, Jeffrey, Johnson, Lewis and Clark, McConaughy, Sutherland, Swanson

Trees: ash, basswood, box elder, cedar, cottonwood, elm, hackberry, locust, oak, pine, walnut, willow

Wild Plants: blue flag, buffalo grass, chokecherry, columbine, evening primrose, goldenrod, grama grass, larkspur, phlox, poppy, spiderwort, violet, wild plum, wild rose

Animals: badger, coyote, elk, mule deer, muskrat, opossum, prairie dog, pronghorn, rabbit, raccoon, skunk, squirrel

Birds: bald eagle, cardinal, chickadee, duck, flicker, goose, heron, pheasant, plover, purple finch, quail, sandhill crane, wild turkey, woodpecker

Fish: bass, carp, catfish, crappie, perch, pike, trout

Endangered Animals: black-footed ferret, blacknose shiner, Eskimo curlew, least tern, pallid sturgeon, piping plover, sturgeon chub, swift fox, Topeka shiner, whooping crane

Endangered Plants: blowout penstemon, Colorado butterfly plant, saltwort

Black-footed ferret

TIMELINE

Nebraska History

1500s Pawnee Indians migrate to what is now Nebraska from farther south.

1682 Explorer René-Robert Cavelier, Sieur de La Salle, claims the lands drained by the Mississippi River for France. The region, later known as the Louisiana Territory, includes present-day Nebraska.

1700s Arapaho, Cheyenne, Omaha, Oto, Ponca, and Lakota Indians thrive in what is now Nebraska.

1739 Frenchmen Pierre and Paul Mallet become the first Europeans known to cross Nebraska.

1762 Louisiana Territory is given to Spain.

1800 Louisiana Territory is given back to France.

1803 The United States gains Nebraska as part of the Louisiana Purchase.

1804 Explorers Meriwether Lewis and William Clark lead the U.S. government's first expedition through Nebraska.

1819–1820 The U.S. Army builds Fort Atkinson, its first post in present-day Nebraska and the first west of the Mississippi River, to protect the frontier.

1823 Fur traders found Bellevue, Nebraska's first town.

1843 Great numbers of pioneers heading for the Far West begin traveling across Nebraska on the Oregon Trail.

1854 The U.S. Congress establishes Nebraska Territory; Missouri, Oto, and Omaha Indians give up lands and move to reservations; Nebraska Territory opens to settlement.

1863 Daniel Freeman is the first person to file a claim under the Homestead Act, settling near Beatrice, Nebraska.

1865 The Union Pacific Railroad starts building the eastern end of the first railroad from the Missouri River to the West Coast, beginning at Omaha.

1867 Nebraska becomes the thirty-seventh state.

1874–1877 Huge swarms of grasshoppers descend on Nebraska, destroying crops and causing many settlers to lose their farms.

1890–1900 Nebraska's Populist Party fights for agricultural reforms.

1892 Mathew O. Ricketts becomes the first black person to serve in the state legislature.

1904 Congress passes the Kinkaid Homestead Act, which promotes settlement in the Sandhills and the Panhandle.

1929 The Great Depression begins.

1939 Petroleum is discovered in southeastern Nebraska, helping the state recover from the Great Depression.

1942 Kingsley Dam is completed on the North Platte River, forming Lake McConaughy.

1948 The Strategic Air Command sets up headquarters at Offutt Air Force Base, bringing thousands of jobs to Nebraska.

1966–1969 Race riots erupt in Omaha.

1967 Nebraskans vote to adopt a sales tax and an income tax.

1980s Many farms are sold, which refocuses Nebraska's economy on small industries.

1986 Nebraska is the first state to have two women candidates for governor: Kay Orr and Helen Boosalis; Kay Orr is elected the nation's first Republican female governor.

1990 The state government passes a major tax increase to fund public education.

1992 Nebraskans vote to adopt a state lottery.

1997 State lawmakers select "A Place Like Nebraska" as the state song and the channel catfish as the state fish.

1998 State legislators choose milk as the state beverage; the first electricity-producing wind turbines in the state are installed in Springview.

2005 The U.S. Strategic Command (STRATCOM) replaces the Strategic Air Command (SAC) and introduces technology that launches Omaha as a national telecommunications center.

2006 Nebraska claims the top three beef cattle counties in the United States, including the country's number one, Cherry County.

2008 *Forbes* magazine rates Omaha's Warren Buffett, who runs Berkshire Hathaway, the wealthiest person in the world; the Thurston County board enacts a law making American Indian Day a county-paid holiday on the fourth Monday of September; the state's safe-haven law goes into effect and is refined to protect from prosecution only parents of infants up to thirty days old whom they abandon.

ECONOMY

Agricultural Products: beef cattle, chickens, corn, dry beans, grain sorghum, hay, hogs, oats, potatoes, sheep, soybeans, sugar beets, wheat

Sugar beets

Manufactured Products: aircraft equipment, electronics components, food products, machinery, metal products, television parts, tires

Natural Resources: limestone, petroleum, sand and gravel

Business and Trade: banking, insurance, real estate, telecommunications, tourism

CALENDAR OF CELEBRATIONS

Crane-Fest Each spring more than 500,000 migrating sandhill and whooping cranes stop to feed near the Platte River on their way north. Two great places to spot them are Rowe Sanctuary and Fort Kearny.

Arbor Day Celebration

Nebraska City goes all out for Arbor Day, the holiday founded by its resident J. Sterling Morton to encourage the planting of trees. The April festival includes a tree giveaway, hands-on craft demonstrations, and a parade.

Lady Vestey Victorian Festival

Nebraska celebrity Evelene Brodstone grew up in tiny Superior, traveled to China as secretary for the Vestey meatpacking company, then married the company boss, who was also an English lord. In May her hometown remembers her with a nineteenth-century costume parade and a formal afternoon tea.

Arbor Day Celebration

Nebraskaland Days Each June, North Platte celebrates Nebraska's frontier spirit with a nine-day blowout featuring country music and dancing, barbecues, and the rough-and-ready Buffalo Bill Rodeo.

Omaha Summer Arts Festival Creativity is the theme of this June celebration. You can try your hand at painting or jewelry making, or even learn how to perform magic.

Nebraska's Big Rodeo Held each July in Burwell, this action-packed event features chuck wagon races, steer wrestling, bull riding, and a longhorn cattle show.

Nebraska's Big Rodeo

Wilber Czech Festival The polka bands at this August celebration in Wilber will have visitors dancing in no time. If their feet get tired, they can rest awhile and eat some *kolache* or check out the parades of Czech costumes.

Nebraska State Fair Farmers from every county in the state show off crops and livestock at the end of the summer in Lincoln.

Kass Kounty King Korn Karnival Plattsmouth kicks off this September festival by crowning a local couple king and queen of "Kornland." The royal pair presides over ugly-pickup and slow-tractor contests, firefighter water fights, and three big parades.

Nebraska State Fair

Old West Days Buckaroos from far and wide hit town for this three-day shindig in Valentine, held on the first weekend in October. Festivities include a horse parade, cowboy poetry readings, old-time stage shows, and an American-Indian powwow.

Light of the World Pageant Since 1946 Minden has ushered in the holiday season with an outdoor Christmas pageant performed by local citizens. As thousands of onlookers brave the cold, the county courthouse flickers in a display of ten thousand lights.

STATE STARS

Grover Cleveland Alexander (1887–1950) was one of the most winning pitchers in baseball history. Born in Elba, Alexander joined the major leagues in 1911 as a pitcher for the Philadelphia Phillies. After pitching a whopping ninety lifetime shutouts and winning 373 games, in 1938 he was elected to the Baseball Hall of Fame.

Fred Astaire (1899–1987) was a Hollywood dancer whose lighthearted elegance was world renowned. Born in Omaha, Astaire took dancing lessons at an early age and gave his first New York stage performance when he was seven. He later danced his way through dozens of movie musicals, including ten with his best-known partner, Ginger Rogers. *Top Hat* and *Swing Time* are among his many beloved films.

Fred Astaire

Max A. Baer (1909–1959), a native of Omaha, was a hard-hitting boxer who knocked out more than fifty opponents during his twelve-year career. In 1934 Baer beat Italian bruiser Primo Carnera to become the heavyweight champion of the world. Baer might have kept his title longer, but he loved being in the spotlight more than he liked training. While clowning around in the ring, he lost to the less-talented James Braddock in 1935.

Max A. Baer

Marlon Brando (1924–2004) was an actor who shot to stardom playing tough characters living in a harsh world. Brando got his start at the Community Playhouse in Omaha, the city in which he was born. In 1947 he made a big impact on Broadway in the play *A Streetcar Named Desire*. He later turned to Hollywood, where his riveting performances in *On the Waterfront* and *The Godfather* brought him two Academy Awards.

William Jennings Bryan (1860–1925) was one of America's most brilliant public speakers. As a lawyer in Lincoln, he became active in the Populist Revolt, a movement to make conditions better for farmers. Bryan ran for president three times and spoke out often for the rights of working people. He was later a prosecutor in the famous Scopes trial, a court case in which a teacher named John Scopes was tried for teaching the theory of evolution.

Johnny Carson (1925–2005) was the longtime host of the television program *The Tonight Show*. Carson moved with his family to Norfolk when he was eight years old, and he studied speech and radio at the University of Nebraska. After working as a radio announcer in Omaha, he headed for Hollywood, where his appearance on America's favorite late-night talk show made him a household name.

Johnny Carson

Willa Cather (1873–1947)
was a writer whose works paint
a vivid picture of life on the
western plains. Cather moved
to Nebraska with her family
when she was nine. While living
in Webster County and Red
Cloud, she fell in love with the
prairie. She later captured its
drama in widely read novels
such as *My Ántonia* and
O Pioneers!

Willa Cather

William F. "Buffalo Bill" Cody (1846–1917) was a legendary cowboy
entertainer. Cody settled in Nebraska Territory with his family when
he was eight and became a Pony Express rider at age fourteen. After
earning his nickname hunting buffalo, he traveled to New York,
where he demonstrated his frontier skills onstage. Buffalo Bill's own
extravagant Wild West shows, which started in Omaha in 1883,
toured the United States and Europe for thirty years.

Crazy Horse (1842–1877) was a visionary Lakota leader whose bold
resistance to the U.S. government made him a legend in his own time.
Crazy Horse grew up hunting buffalo on the Nebraska plains. In a
fierce battle to defend Lakota freedom in 1876, he defeated General
George Armstrong Custer at the Battle of the Little Bighorn. He was
killed at Fort Robinson the following year.

Ruth Etting (1897–1978) was known in the 1920s and 1930s as America's Sweetheart of Song. Born in David City, she rose to fame in Chicago, where she met and married a gangster who managed her career. "Button Up Your Overcoat" and "Ten Cents a Dance" were among her most popular songs.

Ruth Etting

Edward Joseph Flanagan

Edward Joseph Flanagan (1886–1948) founded Boys Town, a
   community where homeless and troubled boys could live, work, and
   learn. A Catholic priest who was born in Ireland, Flanagan moved to
   Nebraska in 1912. He created an entire village for needy boys outside
   of Omaha, with its own chapel, post office, gymnasium, and school.

Henry Fonda (1905–1982), who was born in Grand Island and grew up in Omaha, was one of the most popular movie stars of the 1940s and 1950s. Fonda was shy as a boy, and it wasn't until he was twenty that he tried out for his first play. He eventually moved to Hollywood, where his quiet good looks propelled him to fame in such films as *The Grapes of Wrath* and *12 Angry Men*. At the end of his career, Fonda won an Academy Award for his performance in *On Golden Pond*.

Henry Fonda

Gerald R. Ford (1913–2006), born in Omaha as Leslie King Jr., served as president of the United States from 1974 to 1977. A U.S. congressman from Michigan for twenty-five years, Ford became vice president after Spiro T. Agnew resigned from office in 1973. When President Richard M. Nixon also resigned, Ford took his place, helping the nation recover after Nixon's presidency was tarnished by the Watergate political scandal.

Gerald R. Ford

Bob Gibson (1935–) was a baseball great whose pitching, batting, and fielding talents were unparalleled. During his childhood in Omaha, Gibson suffered from rickets and asthma, but that didn't stop him from playing ball. He joined the St. Louis Cardinals in 1959, and within a decade, he had chalked up three thousand strikeouts, something only one other player had done before.

Bob Gibson

Joyce C. Hall (1891–1982), who grew up in David City and Norfolk, founded Hallmark Cards. At age eighteen, Hall launched a mail-order postcard business from his room at a YMCA in Kansas City. Five years later he opened a greeting-card plant with his brothers, which grew into the megacompany Hallmark. In 1957 Hall received the Horatio Alger Award for working his way from rags to riches.

Susette La Flesche (1854–1903), a member of the Omaha tribe, was a teacher, writer, and public speaker who led a campaign for the rights of American Indians. La Flesche was educated at white-run boarding schools, and she moved easily between the white and the Indian worlds. In 1879 she traveled the country, speaking out on behalf of the Ponca tribe, who had been forced to leave their Nebraska lands.

Malcolm X (1925–1965), born Malcolm Little, was one of the most controversial figures of the civil rights era. The son of a black Baptist preacher living in Omaha, he saw racial injustice at an early age. He later found inspiration in the Nation of Islam and gave passionate speeches against the evils of white power. Malcolm X was murdered in New York City in 1965.

John G. Neihardt (1881–1973) was an award-winning poet who found inspiration in the culture of Nebraska's American Indians. Neihardt's best-known work, *Black Elk Speaks*, grew out of conversations he had with a Lakota elder. Neihardt lived in Bancroft and Cuming County.

Tillie Olsen (1912–2007), a writer, was born and raised in Omaha. A child of the Depression, Olsen never finished high school; and the responsibilities of work and family kept her from writing for many years. Today her short stories are widely read and admired for their emotional power. Olsen received an O. Henry Award for her story "Tell Me a Riddle," which was later made into an Academy Award–winning film.

Edwin E. Perkins (1889–1961) invented Kool-Aid. Perkins started concocting soft drinks at the age of eleven in Hendley using a kit he ordered from a magazine. Soon he was running his own mail-order business, and the fruit-flavored beverage syrup he sold was great in demand. To cut shipping costs, in 1927 he converted the syrup into powder. Kool-Aid was an instant hit and still is—worldwide, more than 500 million gallons are consumed each year.

Red Cloud (1822–1909) was one of the Lakota's most revered warriors and statesmen, who battled the U.S. takeover of Indian land and later worked to preserve the power of chiefs on reservations.

Mari Sandoz (1896–1966) was a writer known for her vivid descriptions of life on the Nebraska plains. Her many novels, histories, and biographies give an honest account of the violent conflicts that divided homesteaders, buffalo hunters, and American Indians, as well as the joys they experienced in a beautiful land. Her best-known work is *Old Jules*, a biography of her father.

Standing Bear (1829–1908), a leader of the Ponca tribe, launched a landmark protest to help his people regain their traditional lands. In 1877 the Ponca were forced to move from Nebraska to Oklahoma (then Indian Territory), where more than a third of them died the first year. Standing Bear spoke out for the right to return home to bury his son's remains; and in a groundbreaking court case, his voice was finally heard.

Darryl Zanuck (1902–1979) was the producer of such classic films as *How Green Was My Valley* and *All About Eve* and cofounder of the film company Twentieth Century Fox. Zanuck started making movies in the 1920s, and in 1927 he produced the world's first talking picture, *The Jazz Singer*. Known as one of the most talented producers in show business, he later won three Oscars. Zanuck was born in Wahoo.

Red Cloud

TOUR THE STATE

Chimney Rock National Historic Site (Bayard) This towering landmark on the Oregon Trail can be seen from 30 miles away. The visitors' center tells of the many settlers who passed by it on their westward journey.

Joslyn Art Museum (Omaha) You can see some of the nineteenth and twentieth century's most beautiful American and European art in this world-class gallery. Built in 1931 with thirty-eight different kinds of marble, the museum itself is a work of art.

Joslyn Art Museum

Museum of Nebraska History (Lincoln) This three-story museum contains everything from moon rocks to a replica of a small-town Nebraska store.

Scotts Bluff National Monument (Gering) Visitors can drive or climb to the top of this bluff for amazing views of the North Platte River valley and the Oregon-California Trail.

Buffalo Bill Ranch State Historical Park (North Platte) After touring cowboy legend Buffalo Bill's ranch, you can get in the saddle yourself for a trail ride around the grounds.

Buffalo Bill Ranch State Historical Park

Museum of the Fur Trade (Chadron) The first Europeans who came to Nebraska made a living trapping and trading in furs. Located on the site of an original trading post once owned by the American Fur Company, this

Museum of the Fur Trade

museum sheds light on the lives of fur traders in North America and their American-Indian business partners.

Sidney Downtown Historic District (Sidney) Wild West legends such as Calamity Jane and Wild Bill Hickok used to pass through Sidney, a regular stop on the Union Pacific Railroad. A stroll downtown takes modern-day visitors past old-time shops, theaters, and saloons once frequented by pioneers and gold seekers.

Stuhr Museum of the Prairie Pioneer (Grand Island) This indoor-outdoor living history museum offers a tour through a blacksmith's shop, an old-fashioned railroad station, and a Pawnee Indian lodge, with guides in period costume.

Stuhr Museum of the Prairie Pioneer

Arbor Lodge State Historical Park and Arboretum (Nebraska City) The fifty-two-room mansion in this park was once the home of Julius Sterling Morton, the founder of Arbor Day. Visitors can tour the lavish house and arboretum, featuring more than 250 kinds of trees.

National Museum of Roller Skating (Lincoln) This one-of-a-kind museum traces the history of roller skating back to its beginnings in the early 1700s. Learn how sports such as roller hockey, roller polo, and even roller basketball have changed with the evolution of the roller skate.

Fort Niobrara National Wildlife Refuge (Valentine) Nature trails wind through 19,000 acres populated with buffalo, elk, and more than two hundred species of birds.

Fort Niobrara National Wildlife Refuge

Nebraska National Forest (Halsey and Valentine) In 1902 Nebraskans set out to increase the state's woodlands by planting trees in the Sandhills. They created the largest forest in the Western Hemisphere made by human hands.

Ashfall Fossil Beds State Historical Park (Royal) Around 10 million years ago, a volcanic eruption left the marshes of northern Nebraska buried in 8 feet of ash. This incredible site offers a close-up view of the fossilized remains of hundreds of prehistoric creatures caught in the fallout.

Carhenge and Car Art Reserve (Alliance) Created in 1987, this outdoor sculpture made of old cars duplicates Stonehenge, a prehistoric stone circle constructed in England; however, creator Jim Renders made this circle from spray-painted, junked autos.

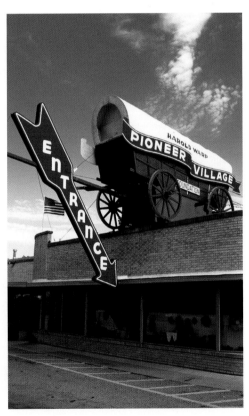

Harold Warp Pioneer Village (Minden) Old-time objects from antique tractors to china teacups are on display in this fascinating frontier museum of Americana. Its twenty-eight historic buildings include a genuine Pony Express relay station, a one-room schoolhouse, and a sod house.

Harold Warp Pioneer Village

Museum of Nebraska Art (Kearney) This museum highlights artworks created in Nebraska from the early days of exploration through today.

Fort Robinson State Park (Crawford) Visitors to Nebraska's largest state park can hike through pine forests, travel by stagecoach, and even sample buffalo stew. Its historic buildings recall the days when the U.S. Army clashed with American Indians.

Agate Fossil Beds National Monument (Harrison) Thousands of fossils lie buried in this prehistoric graveyard. Trails will take you past those that have been uncovered—many still resting where they were found.

Agate Fossil Beds National Monument

Toadstool Geologic Park

Girls and Boys Town (Omaha) Founded in 1917 as Boys Town, this historic home for troubled children now welcomes both girls and boys. Drop by and either take a self-guided tour or ask a student guide to show you around town.

Toadstool Geologic Park (Crawford) The sandstone in this section of the Oglala National Grassland has been eroded by wind and water to form weird, mushroomlike shapes.

FUN FACTS

The largest elephant fossil ever discovered was found in south-central Nebraska.

The nation's first transcontinental highway, Lincoln Highway (now Route 30), cuts across Nebraska.

The Union Pacific Railroad line between North Platte and Gibbon is the world's busiest stretch of rail for freight trains, with more than 130 trains passing through every twenty-four hours.

Roosevelt Park in Hebron boasts one of the world's largest swings. The seat has room for about thirty-two kids and is 32 feet long.

Kool-Aid, chicken pot pies, and the Reuben sandwich were invented in Nebraska.

Dannebrog, Nebraska, boasts the National Liars Hall of Fame, founded by author and television celebrity Roger Welsch.

Nebraska is the only state in which all electric power facilities are publicly owned. It has no private power companies.

Find Out More

If you want to find out more about Nebraska, check your local library or bookstore for these titles.

GENERAL STATE BOOKS

Brown, Jonathan. *Nebraska* (Portraits of the States). Milwaukee, WI: Gareth Stevens, 2006.

Sanders, Doug. *Nebraska* (It's My State!). New York: Marshall Cavendish Benchmark, 2006.

Zollman, Pam. *Nebraska* (Rookie Read-About Geography). New York: Children's Press, 2007.

SPECIAL INTEREST BOOKS

Clements, Andrew. *Room One: A Mystery or Two.* New York: Scholastic, 2006.

Enss, Chris. *The Doctor Wore Petticoats: Women Physicians of the Old West.* Guilford, CT: TwoDot, 2006.

Josephy, Alvin. *Lewis and Clark Through Indian Eyes.* New York: Knopf, 2006.

Keating, Frank. *The Trial of Standing Bear*. Oklahoma City, OK: Oklahoma Heritage Association, 2008.

Meltzer, Milton. *Willa Cather: A Biography*. Minneapolis, MN: Twenty-First Century Books, 2007.

Pringle, Lawrence. *American Slave, American Hero: York of the Lewis and Clark Expedition*. Honesdale, PA: Calkins Creek, 2006.

WEBSITES

Nebraska State Government

www.nebraska.gov

The official Nebraska government website contains facts and links to state agencies.

Nebraska State Historical Society

www.nebraskahistory.org

This site contains state history records and links to pioneer diaries, photographs, and more.

Nebraska Studies

www.nebraskastudies.org

The studies available through this site detail the state and its people from pre–1500 to the present, with a timeline, stories, photos, and historic documents.

Index

Page numbers in **boldface** are illustrations and charts.

ABOUT THE AUTHORS

Ruth Bjorklund is a former children's librarian. She lives on Bainbridge Island, near Seattle, Washington, with her husband, two children, three cats, and two dogs.

Marlee Richards is an award-winning author of more than sixty-five books for readers of all ages. She has written about many different topics, from history and biography to tooth fairies, raising kids, and the Pony Express. Her favorite topics allow her to play detective to find new and interesting facts for her readers. For the Celebrate the States series she interviews people from the state and investigates new regions of the country.